The School Mental Health Response Handbook

by the same author

Building Happiness, Resilience and Motivation in Adolescents
A Positive Psychology Curriculum for Well-Being
Ruth MacConville and Tina Rae
ISBN 978 1 84905 261 0
eISBN 978 0 85700 548 9

of related interest

The Mentally Healthy Schools Workbook
Practical Tips, Ideas, Action Plans and Worksheets
for Making Meaningful Change
Pooky Knightsmith
Foreword by Norman Lamb
ISBN 978 1 78775 148 4
eISBN 978 1 78775 149 1

Essential Listening Skills for Busy School Staff
What to Say When You Don't Know What to Say
Nick Luxmoore
ISBN 978 1 84905 565 9
eISBN 978 1 78450 000 9

The Mental Health and Wellbeing Handbook for Schools
Clare Erasmus
Foreword by Chris Edwards
ISBN 978 1 78592 481 1
eISBN 978 1 78450 869 2

THE SCHOOL MENTAL HEALTH RESPONSE HANDBOOK

Practical Strategies for Educators and Support Staff

Ali D'Amario and Tina Rae

Jessica Kingsley Publishers
London and Philadelphia

First published in Great Britain in 2025 by Jessica Kingsley Publishers
An imprint of John Murray Press

1

A CIP catalogue record for this title is available from the
British Library and the Library of Congress

ISBN 978 1 80501 386 0
eISBN 978 1 80501 387 7

Printed and bound in Great Britain by CPI Group

Jessica Kingsley Publishers' policy is to use papers that are natural,
renewable and recyclable products and made from wood grown in
sustainable forests. The logging and manufacturing processes are expected
to conform to the environmental regulations of the country of origin.

Jessica Kingsley Publishers
Carmelite House
50 Victoria Embankment
London EC4Y 0DZ
www.jkp.com

John Murray Press
Part of Hodder & Stoughton Ltd
An Hachette Company

The authorised representative in the EEA is Hachette Ireland,
8 Castlecourt Centre, Dublin 15, D15 XTP3, Ireland (email: info@hbgi.ie)

Contents

Acknowledgements

We would like to thank all at Jessica Kingsley Publishers, especially Elen Griffiths, Maudisa King, Will Moran and Laura Savage, for sharing our passion and bringing to life our vision for this publication.

We would also like to thank our families and friends for their love, kindness and patience, always, but especially during the writing of this book.

Most of all, we owe a debt of gratitude to the incredible educators we have both worked with over the years. The patience, compassion and love you provide to the pupils you work with, often in challenging circumstances, is the inspiration for this handbook.

'They may forget what you said, but they will never forget how you made them feel.' – attributed to Carl W. Buehner

About the Authors

Dr Ali D'Amario is an independent Educational and Child Psychologist. She has over 15 years' experience working in education, having previously been a teacher in a secondary school. Within her role, she works strategically with schools and multi-academy trusts (MATs), developing whole-school mental health provision, training and supervising emotional literacy support assistants (ELSAs), supporting the implementation of Nurture Groups and delivering staff training and parent workshops. She also works with children at a group and individual level, specializing in supporting emotional wellbeing and mental health. In response to the increased need to empower school staff with an understanding of mental health needs and how to respond safely and effectively, she developed the mental health response protocol, the FIRES Framework. This was the inspiration for this publication and is referred to extensively throughout.

Ali studied for her doctorate at the University of East London under the supervision of Dr Tina Rae, whom she credits for instilling in her a passion for supporting the wellbeing of children, young people, school staff and families. Ali is proud to be on the editorial advisory board for the NurtureUK publication International Journal of Nurture in Education and is a wellbeing consultant for the children's mental health charity The Bee-lieve Foundation. Ali previously co-authored *Philosophy for Children: The Man in the Moon* (2014), the *Recovery Toolbox for Wellbeing* series (2021) and *Promoting Positive Body Image in Teenagers* (2021) with Dr Tina Rae.

@AliDamarioEP
www.alidamariopsychology.com

Dr Tina Rae has 40 years' experience working with children, adults and families in clinical and educational contexts within local authorities and specialist services. She is currently working as a Consultant Educational and Child Psychologist in a range of SEMH and mainstream contexts and for fostering agencies as a Consultant Psychologist supporting foster carers, social workers and looked after children. She was an Academic and Professional tutor for the Doctorate in Educational and Child Psychology (University of East London) from 2010 to 2016. She is a registered member of the Health and Care Professions Council, a member of the European Network for Social and Emotional Competence, a former trustee of NurtureUK and a former member of the advisory boards for Fresh Start in Education and for the Association for Child and Adolescent Mental Health (ACAMH).

Tina is a prolific author and has over 100 publications to date. These reflect her ongoing passion for developing practical resources for schools that have an evidence base and that enable practitioners to ethically deliver effective preventative mental health interventions in schools. Recent publications include the following:

Rae, T. (2023) *Understanding and Supporting Refugee Children and Young People: A Practical Resource for Teachers, Parents and Carers and Those Exposed to the Trauma of War.* London: Routledge.

Rae, T. (2022) *The Bereavement Book: Activities to Support Children and Young People Through Grief and Loss.* Buckingham: Hinton House.

Rae, T. & D'Amario, A. (2021) *Promoting Positive Body Image in Teenagers: A Programme of Essential Strategies and Resources.* Buckingham: Hinton House.

Rae, T. & D'Amario, A. (2021) *A Recovery Toolbox of Wellbeing in the Early Years for Children Aged 3–6.* Buckingham: Hinton House.

Rae, T. (2020) *Supporting Children and Young People with Emotionally Based School Avoidance.* Buckingham: Hinton House.

Rae, T., Middleton, T. & Walshe, J. (2020) *Nurturing Peer Supervision: Supporting the Wellbeing of Those Who Nurture.* Glasgow: NurtureUK.

Rae, T. (2020) *It's OK Not to Be OK: A Guide to Wellbeing.* London: QED Publishing.

Rae, T., Such, A. & Wood, J. (2020) *The Well Being Tool Kit for Mental Health Leads in Schools: A Comprehensive Training Resource to Support Emotional Wellbeing in Education and Social Care.* Buckingham: Hinton House.

Tina is a regular speaker at national and international conferences and events, providing training courses and supervision for school-based staff in both special and mainstream contexts and educational psychology services across the UK and internationally.

@DrTinarae

Preface

'I have been a TA for 12 years now and love the job because I get to work with young people and know I am making a difference when I support them, but the job has changed and I'm now doing more support for those children who have anxiety, panic attacks and really some very traumatic backgrounds. It is very different now, and I definitely see more mental health problems, which makes me feel inadequate at times, and stressed, as we have never really had the sort of training to deal with all this stuff – just the odd session here and there from our EP. We need more. I need to feel that I am not doing harm, and the right thing, so having our own training and stuff would be helpful right now – especially from people who really understand our role as it stands now.' (Emma, teaching assistant)

'When I get home late afternoons, I often feel worried about some of the kids I spoke to during the day. There is not always time to go and see our mental health lead to get advice, and I honestly think we are dealing with stuff that is really complicated. I get stressed when kids are saying they're going to self-harm or feeling really down and depressed. I obviously report back to our designated safeguarding lead but am still left feeling concerned and anxious.' (Shaheen, teacher)

'I think all school staff need specific training in mental health because this is now part of our job, like it or not. I do like it because I feel that I can make a difference, but that is down to the fact that we get good supervision. Now, when people are new to working in education, I think they need more bespoke training in mental health needs so that they feel confident and don't get overly stressed.' (Gordon, emotional literacy support assistant)

At the time of writing this handbook, it is clear that schools across the UK are coping with a mental health crisis, with school leaders in primary and secondary schools reporting a rise in anxiety, depression, self-harm and eating disorders amongst their pupils. Mental health services are struggling to cope with the demand, leading to long wait times for support. The impact of the COVID-19 pandemic cannot be overstated in terms of its contribution to the deterioration in mental health for many children and adults alike, and we must be careful not to overlook the potential for symptoms of trauma to be displayed over many years to come.

The *Good Childhood Report* (Children's Society 2021) looked at the impact of COVID-19 and found that, while most have coped relatively well with the upheaval and disruption of the pandemic, an estimated quarter of a million have struggled. Those who indicated that they had not coped well with the COVID-19 lockdowns were also found to have low levels of wellbeing. Three in five parents said that the pandemic had had a negative impact on their children's education, and almost two in five of the children taking part in the survey were less happy with their progress with schoolwork than before. It is now evident that the many restrictions and lockdowns enforced during the pandemic have impacted those areas that we know are important to wellbeing. Therefore, we must ensure that wherever possible, children have opportunities and are encouraged to connect, be active, be creative, keep learning and take notice.

The more recent cost-of-living crisis has meant that one in four children in the UK are living in poverty (Barnardo's, 2022), meaning that in some cases, the basic needs of being fed, being warm and feeling safe are not able to be met. In the survey by Barnardo's, 26 percent of parents felt that their child's mental health had worsened due to the cost-of-living crisis. Additionally, according to UNICEF (2022), the number of countries experiencing war and conflict is at its highest in 30 years. The media is currently awash with horrifying stories about children being targeted by attacks, making the world feel like an unsafe and frightening place. We are welcoming children to our schools who have fled from war zones and have experienced significant trauma for which they will require our love, support and a level of expertise that goes beyond that taught during initial teacher training.

We know that children in the UK are becoming more unhappy. The annual *Good Childhood Report* from the Children's Society (2023) found that children are now significantly less happy with school, family relationships, their appearance and life in general than when the survey started in 2009. According to the survey, unhappiness with school, appearance and the future peaks at age 15. There is also another noticeable increase at the age of 12 following the transition to secondary school. Not only are our children becoming more unhappy, but a study comparing the wellbeing of children in the UK with other European countries (OECD, 2019) found that Britain ranked last for children feeling an overall sense of purpose in life. Britain was only beaten by Malta in the measure of the saddest children in Europe.

Something needs to change.

The 2023 *Good Childhood Report* highlights the fact that early intervention needs to be a key goal, but also that one of the biggest challenges in delivering this is the lack of appropriate funding. The annual report on children's services funding by Action for Children, Barnardo's, NSPCC, National Children's Bureau and the Children's Society (Children's Services Funding Alliance, 2021) highlights this. Since 2010, local authorities have had to make reductions in spend of 48 percent in early intervention services while also having to increase spending on crisis provision, such as children's care services and youth justice, by 38 percent.

So, what does this mean for those of us who support children and young people at a school-based level?

Increasingly, with tight budgets, preventative work undertaken at the school-based level is a key focus. This is particularly important when mental health services are so stretched and specialist support is frequently unavailable to those in need. The mental health leads in schools, along with SENCos and designated safeguarding leads, are shaping whole-school approaches to mental health and wellbeing. At the ground level, those who are frequently asked to support children and young people with mental health difficulties, both individually and in small-group contexts, are teaching assistants or learning support assistants.

For many, the traditional teaching assistant (TA) role has now taken on a significantly different aspect in terms of supporting children with learning and behaviour – that of supporting the child or young person dealing with a range of mental health issues, including, among others, anxiety, eating disorders, depression, self-harm and panic attacks. This role has been further reinforced and highlighted during the COVID-19 pandemic. TAs are often the ones supporting children and young people when they are most distressed and dysregulated, with recent research highlighting the verbal and physical abuse frequently endured by many (Holt & Birchall, 2022). Even well before the pandemic, a survey suggested that 53 percent of TAs had experienced physical violence from pupils during the previous year (UNISON, 2016).

In our view, this is a big ask. Most school staff have concerns that they do not have the knowledge base or skill set to support children in this more therapeutic way effectively. There is also a concern that appropriate support and supervision systems are not always in place to support staff effectively following difficult, emotive and often high-stakes situations. *Understanding that you are not being asked to be a therapist or provide therapeutic intervention is essential.* However, it is also clearly imperative that school staff develop an appropriate skill set and knowledge base to engage therapeutically in supporting children with these complex needs and issues.

This is, in essence, the rationale for developing this handbook. We want it to become a go-to resource for anyone working in schools. Given that there are now estimated to be five children with a diagnosable mental health issue in every class of 30 children, all school staff need to feel confident and empowered to support these needs. This comes at a time when school budgets are stretched and often unable to cover costly training courses. This resource will support educators in effectively engaging with children and young people at both a preventative level and in recognizing and responding to mental health needs as they arise. We wanted to ensure this is an easy-to-navigate resource and have presented it in a user-friendly format. We have included the key topics that we think most school staff will encounter in their work, and therefore need to focus on, and have provided information sheets, top tips and key strategies or approaches that can be used effectively. We have used our knowledge of evidence-based approaches and practical applications to ensure that this truly is a valuable and well-informed resource.

Of course, we may have missed something! There is so much that we could have included. However, we were also mindful that we did not want to overload practitioners and present them with a resource that is too complex or overwhelming in terms of content and volume.

If you are an educator responding to the mental health needs of a child or young person, we hope that this handbook will provide you with a positive, practical framework and ensure that you gain the confidence needed to develop your practice further, while also pointing you in the right direction to seek additional support, information or training in each of the key areas.

We feel very strongly that supporting children and young people's mental health and wellbeing is one of the most critical roles currently undertaken in school contexts. This has to be our priority, and our ability to build strong, positive relationships lies at the heart of everything we do. Learning how to be the key adult who responds therapeutically, understands the impact of trauma, knows how to listen, can emotionally coach and create a safe space, and can be curious, understanding and empathic are all key elements of such relationships. We hope this resource will guide you in developing such relationships and build your confidence in supporting children and young people at both the preventative and reactive levels. Clearly, we would like the focus to be mainly on preventative work. However, we are also aware that there will be an ongoing need for responses to significant distress for those at risk of engaging in self-harming behaviours or suicide.

Ultimately, the purpose is to ensure that you feel safe in undertaking your role and can deliver appropriate interventions ethically in the knowledge that you understand your boundaries and can access appropriate additional support to reflect on and process your work.

References

Barnardo's (2022) *At What Cost? The Impact of the Cost-of-living Crisis on Children and Young People.* www.barnardos.org.uk/sites/default/files/2022-10/At%20what%20cost_impact%20of%20cost%20of%20living%20final%20report.pdf

Children's Services Funding Alliance (2021) *Children and Young People's Services: Spending 2010–11 to 2019–20.* www.barnardos.org.uk/sites/default/files/2021-07/Spending%20on%20children%27s%20services%20in%20England%20-%20July%202021.pdf

Children's Society (2021) *Good Childhood Report/* www.childrenssociety.org.uk/information/professionals/resources/good-childhood-report-2021

Children's Society (2023) *Good Childhood Report.* www.childrenssociety.org.uk/sites/default/files/2023-09/The%20Good%20Childhood%20Report%202023.pdf

Holt, A. & Birchall, J. (2022) *Violence towards Teaching/Classroom Assistants in Mainstream UK Schools: Research Findings and Recommendations.* University of Roehampton, UK. www.roehampton.ac.uk/globalassets/documents/research-centres/centre-for-equality-justice-and-social-change/holt-and-birchall-2022-violence-towards-tas.pdf

OECD (2019) *PISA 2018 Results (Volume III): What School Life Means for Students' Lives.* www.oecd.org/education/pisa-2018-results-volume-iii-acd78851-en.html

UNICEF (2022) Children Under Attack. www.unicef.org/children-under-attack

UNISON (2016, 21 June) School support staff facing high levels of violence and abuse, says UNISON | [Press release]. www.unison.org.uk/news/press-release/2016/06/school-support-staff-facing-high-levels-of-violence-and-abuse-says-unison

Introduction

Who is this handbook for?

If you are currently a teacher, a member of senior leadership, part of the pastoral team, a lunchtime supervisor, working in the school office, a mental health lead, a designated safeguarding lead, a SENCo, a learning support assistant, a school counsellor or working in any other role within a school – this handbook is for you! When we experience overwhelming emotions and distress, we seek those with whom we have a relationship, whom we trust, who make us feel safe, and who will listen to us. Unfortunately, this is not always the person in school who has been on a one-day course in supporting mental health needs. All school staff need to be prepared to respond in a safe, effective and supportive way, and it is the responsibility of all staff to know how to recognize signs of possible mental health issues so that intervention can be provided early.

We have tried to make this resource as accessible as possible and to present a range of psychological theories in a commonsense way so that you can see how to apply evidence-based techniques in your daily interactions.

'Every interaction is an intervention.' (Karen Treisman, 2017)

Recognizing how we talk to our children and young people and how we can do this more therapeutically – without actually being a therapist – is a key aim of the resource.

We want you to feel free to dip in and out and to access information at the point of need. For example, if you are working with a young person who is self-harming, your first port of call can be the relevant section of this publication. However, when further sources of help and support are needed, in any of the areas covered in this handbook, you can refer to the 'Where to Get More Help' section, which provides clear information about other resources and services you can access.

We hope you find this useful and supportive and gain confidence when delivering your support to children and young people. We want to ensure that school staff receive both the recognition and the support needed to nurture our most vulnerable children and young people effectively.

Defining mental health

It can be challenging for adults to recognize when a child is experiencing a mental health issue. It can also be difficult for young people to express their feelings and seek much-needed support. However, the research shows us that mental health is an important issue for children. For example, 45 percent of Childline counselling sessions in 2018/19 were related to mental or emotional wellbeing (NSPCC, 2019). Therefore, anyone working with children must be able to recognize the signs and symptoms of a mental health issue and feel confident in supporting and signposting children safely and effectively.

At the outset, as you will see when we introduce the FIRES Framework in Chapter 1, we need to ask the critical question: What do we mean by the term 'mental health'?

> **REFLECTION POINT**
> What is 'mental health'?

Mind (2020) states that mental health is an individual's cognitive, behavioural and emotional wellbeing. We also use the term 'mental health issues' throughout this resource to refer to mental health problems, conditions and mental illnesses. These may or may not be diagnosed.

Commonly, the term 'mental health' is associated with mental illness and therefore, supporting mental health tends to be restricted to the prevention of illness rather than promoting wellbeing (Weare, 2000). The World Health Organization (WHO) use a more positive definition of health, describing it as 'a state of mental well-being that enables people to cope with the stresses of life, realize their abilities, learn well and work well, and contribute to their community' (WHO, 2024).

Consequently, there needs to be a shift from the deficit model of mental health to embracing the notion of positive wellbeing. Within the school context, this would suggest that as well as reacting to mental health challenges and risk factors such as bullying, violence and conflict, there also needs to be a focus on supporting pupils to achieve their goals: to feel loved, to feel safe; to feel joyful; and to care about others (Weare, 2000).

Mental health affects all aspects of a child's development, including their cognitive ability, social skills and emotional wellbeing. For example, Gutman and Vorhaus (2012) found that children with higher levels of emotional, social and behavioural wellbeing have, on average, higher levels of academic achievement. With good mental health, pupils can enjoy childhood and adolescence, cope with stress and adversity, perform better academically and develop positive relationships. Mental health continues to have an important role in adulthood. For example, those with better levels of wellbeing have fewer health issues (Pressman & Cohen, 2005), live longer (Chida & Steptoe, 2008) and are less likely to smoke or abuse alcohol (Deacon et al., 2013).

Who is most at risk?

Any child or young person can experience a mental health issue. In fact, research has shown that around 83 percent of us will experience a diagnosable mental health issue at some point in our lives (Schaefer et al., 2017). Like physical health, mental health changes over time for a variety of reasons.

> 'You can't stop the waves, but you can learn to surf.' (Jon Kabat-Zinn, 2005)

However, the evidence suggests that there are some factors which increase a child's vulnerability and are associated with adverse long-term mental health outcomes.

Abuse and neglect

The trauma caused by abuse and neglect increases the likelihood of children developing a range of mental health difficulties, both during childhood and later in life. These include anxiety, depression, eating disorders and post-traumatic stress disorder (PTSD) (Norman et al., 2012; Widom, 1999).

Certain types of abuse may be connected with specific mental health issues. For example, children who have experienced emotional abuse may be more likely to develop anxiety and depression compared with children who have experienced other types of abuse (Cecil et al., 2017; Gavin, 2011). Lewis et al. (2019) looked at the impact of sexual abuse and found that almost three-quarters (74%) of young people who had experienced sexual assault developed PTSD.

Additional needs and disabilities

Children and young people with additional needs and disabilities may face a range of challenges, including prejudice, discrimination and bullying. These challenges may impact negatively on their self-esteem and sense of belonging, increasing their vulnerability to mental health issues (Faulconbridge, Hunt & Laffan, 2019).

Children from Black, Asian and minority ethnic communities

Children from Black and minority ethnic groups may experience racism, discrimination and prejudice. This can lead to inequalities and issues in accessing appropriate care and support for mental health needs (Race Equality Foundation, 2020).

Life events

Traumatic experiences and stressful situations, such as loss, bereavement or sudden changes in the environment, can trigger mental health issues in some children.

Living in care

Children and young people in the care system are more likely than their peers to experience a mental health issue (NSPCC, 2019). This can be due to isolation and loneliness. Additionally, children in care are likely to have experienced trauma, including loss of relationships, sudden changes, bereavement, neglect or abuse, all of which increase the likelihood of developing a mental health issue (National Youth Advocacy Service, 2019).

LGBTQ+ children and young people

The statistics show that LGBTQ+ children and young people are more vulnerable to experiencing mental health issues. Many reasons have been suggested for this, including prejudice, discrimination, bullying, fear of rejection, and lacking a sense of belonging. These factors and experiences mean they are more likely than their heterosexual and cisgender peers to experience a range of mental health problems (Becerra-Culqui et al., 2018; Chakraborty et al., 2011).

The rise in mental health difficulties

It is now estimated that one in five children have a diagnosable mental health condition; that is six in every class of 30 (NHS, 2023).

The impact of the COVID-19 pandemic cannot be overstated. The massive disruption to two years of education, the loss of opportunities for fun and freedom, the lack of social interaction with friends and family, and the worry about the virus itself have understandably taken their toll on the mental health of some children and young people. A study conducted by the NHS in 2020 revealed that mental health conditions in children had increased by 50 percent in comparison to 2017.

Even before the COVID-19 pandemic, children's mental health services were not able to meet the demand. In 2019, referrals to children's mental health services increased by 35 percent, and the capacity of the service only increased by 4 percent, leaving many children without access to the support that they desperately need (Children's Commissioner, 2021).

The latest data suggests that despite being over the worst of the pandemic, the mental health of children is continuing to deteriorate (NHS, 2023). Most alarmingly, for 17- to 19-year-olds, the proportion with a probable mental health disorder has increased from 1/10 in 2017 to 1/4 in 2023.

Patterns in the data relating to the deterioration of the mental health of children and young people suggest that the downturn in wellbeing began around 2010 (Haidt, 2024). In his book *The Anxious Generation*, Haidt makes a compelling case linking this decline to the popularity of smartphones, and social media in particular.

REFLECTION POINT
What impact has the pandemic had on mental health within your setting?

We also need to be aware that the culture of exams and testing in our schools increases stress levels. In a National Education Union (NEU) survey of teachers, 82 percent said that exams have the most detrimental impact on pupil mental health (Education Executive, 2018).

Statistics tell us that 50 percent of mental health issues are established by the age of 14 and 75 percent by the age of 24 (Kessler et al., 2005). According to Margot Sunderland (2022), research also suggests that, on average, pupils wait ten years to receive support for their mental health needs (Centre for Mental Health, 2016) – and even then, only half of those who seek help get better. These figures, alongside the high numbers of children requiring support and the limitations in the capacity of children's mental health services, lead us to one conclusion: we need to be equipped and confident to identify mental health issues and to provide appropriate support within schools. While school staff cannot be expected to be therapists, there is a real need for emotionally available adults who are able to use therapeutic approaches.

Mental health support in schools

Ofsted's school inspection framework aims to ensure that schools are providing a good education, with supportive pastoral care, to allow students to develop into resilient adults with positive mental health. The framework requires explicitly that students know how to stay mentally healthy (Ofsted, 2023). *Keeping Children Safe in Education* (Department for Education, 2024a) outlines the statutory duty that schools have to promote the welfare of children and young people, including preventing the impairment of their health or development and taking action to enable all children to have the best outcomes. Interestingly, when *Keeping Children Safe in Education* was first published in 2014, the term 'mental health' was mentioned once. At the time of writing this, the most recent update to the guidance mentions the term 'mental health' a total of 44 times, showing the dramatic increase in the government's expectations of schools in this area.

We know from the National Association of Schoolmasters Union of Women Teachers survey that, in 2023, 96 percent of teachers and school leaders stated that they were supporting children and young people who had experienced or were experiencing mental health problems (NASUWT, 2024). Uncoincidentally, a recent survey by the Early Intervention Foundation (2022) found that 98 percent of teachers regard supporting students' mental health and wellbeing as a priority. School staff are in a great position to support wellbeing. This was reinforced in the government Green Paper *Transforming Children and Young People's Mental Health Provision* (Department of Health and Department for Education, 2017), which states:

> There is evidence that appropriately trained and supported staff such as teachers, school nurses, counsellors, and teaching assistants can achieve results comparable to those achieved by trained therapists in delivering a number of interventions addressing mild to moderate mental health problems (such as anxiety, conduct disorder, substance use disorders and post-traumatic stress disorder).

For example, Barrett and Turner (2001) found that teachers were shown to have as much, if not more, positive results than psychologists as group leaders implementing the same intervention for anxious children when they were taught the same techniques and approaches as the psychologists. The suggestion here is not to promote the notion of staff seeking to become or take on the role of 'the therapist' but to recognize that they would be more effective in terms of identifying and preventing the escalation of such difficulties if they were more skilled and knowledgeable in utilizing therapeutic skills and approaches.

We appreciate the many barriers to this. Schools have no money. Staff have no time. Staff are already at breaking point without adding another responsibility. Although many staff feel confident in terms of providing academic and social support to their students, there remains a real concern that they do not have the knowledge base or level of skills required to specifically support those with more complex and emerging mental health difficulties. A TeacherTapp survey by the Early Intervention Foundation in August 2022 found that 43 percent of teachers did not feel confident supporting students with their mental health, and 64 percent of staff had not received training in this area over the last year (EIF, 2022).

The importance of a trauma-informed approach

Margot Sunderland (2022) suggested that schools need to understand the causes behind mental ill-health before they can begin to tackle it. Understanding the emotional pain children and teenagers experience when parents separate – or there is a death in the family or bullying in the school context – is clearly essential, as is the need to ensure that children and young people have safe spaces in which to discuss and process the impact of these experiences.

We know that this idea of 'social buffering', where children and young people have someone who is there for them when they experience these painful moments, who can listen to them, empathize and genuinely understand, really does make all the difference in terms of preventing longer-term mental health issues. As Fonagy (2019) remarks: 'Adversity becomes traumatic when compounded by a sense that one's mind is alone.'

Just one emotionally available adult can make all the difference in a child's life. Without this kind of social buffering, children and young people are at risk of a range of mental health difficulties, academic failure and attendance issues longer term. Burke et al. (2011) identified that children with three or more adverse childhood experiences (ACEs) were three times more likely to fall below the academic expectations, five times more likely to have persistent absence and six times more likely to show distressed behaviour in school. For those with four or more ACEs, more than 50 percent were likely to have learning difficulties and were 32 times more likely to have behaviour problems.

So, everyone in the school community must have an appropriate level of training to identify those at risk and understand some of the symptoms of trauma. We need to be looking for marked changes in terms of concentration or focus, and how some children will retreat into themselves or experience heightened levels of fatigue. It is essential to be observant of all significant symptoms, such as self-isolation and withdrawal from peers or parents, particularly when children and young people are at risk of engaging in self-harm as a means of managing their deep psychological pain.

Many children and young people who had previously experienced mental health difficulties found that the pandemic compounded these issues and resulted in an increase in emotionally based school avoidance (EBSA). Therefore, now, more than ever, we need to ensure that children and young people have access in schools to staff who are emotionally available for them, can listen and empathize, and understand how to approach a conversation about mental health with them. School staff need to know how to build rapport and model ways to self-regulate. Developing these skills, along with curious questioning, validating the child's experiences and not stigmatizing them, are key elements of building such relationships.

This is the main reason we have included a range of key tools and strategies within this resource so that school staff can develop their skill set in using mindfulness techniques, grounding techniques, breathing techniques, and key tools and strategies from cognitive behavioural therapy approaches. In this way, the support is built on the knowledge gained from neuroscientific research. Once we understand the science behind *toxic stress*, we can support a child or young person to move from toxic to *tolerable stress*.

For example, understanding how 'unmourned grief' can trigger withdrawal or 'acting-out' behaviours is essential here, as is recognizing how anxiety can present itself as many different behaviours that some would find challenging in the classroom context. When we understand this and are ready to meet needs in the right way, children can really benefit, processing their past experiences and understanding how they can manage levels of anxiety on a daily basis. Ultimately, they will know they are not alone and have been heard and understood. This is key to ensuring good mental health in the future. In essence, *understanding unmet needs* and *enabling children to understand their emotions* is the key to preventative work, which, in our view, is what we should be all about.

The whole-school approach to mental health

'Schools have an important role to play in supporting the mental health and wellbeing of children by developing whole-school approaches tailored to their particular needs, as well as considering the needs of individual pupils.' (Department for Education, 2018)

A whole-school approach to mental health involves all parts of the school community working together to support the needs of the children. It requires collaboration between senior leaders, all school staff, parents and carers, external agencies and community organizations.

The Department for Education (DfE, 2018) places emphasis on the importance of early intervention when setting out how they envisage the school's role in supporting and promoting mental health and wellbeing:

- *Prevention*: Schools need to create a safe, calm environment where mental health issues are less likely, improving the mental health and wellbeing of the whole school population, and equipping pupils to be resilient so that they can manage the normal stress of life effectively. This will include teaching pupils about mental wellbeing through the curriculum and reinforcing this teaching through school activities and ethos.

- *Identification*: Staff need to be able to identify issues early and accurately.

- *Early support*: Staff need to help pupils to access evidence-based early support and interventions.

- *Access to specialist support*: Schools should work effectively with external agencies to provide swift access or referrals to specialist support and treatment.

They also suggest that schools follow eight key principles to embedding a whole-school approach to mental health and wellbeing (DfE, 2018):

- leadership and management that supports and champions efforts to promote emotional health and wellbeing

- curriculum teaching and learning to promote resilience and support social and emotional learning

- enabling student voice to influence decisions

- staff development to support their own wellbeing and that of students

- identifying need and monitoring impact of interventions

- working with parents and carers

- targeted support and appropriate referral

- an ethos and environment that promotes respect and values diversity.

The role of the senior mental health lead

According to the *Transforming Children and Young People's Mental Health Provision* Green Paper (2017), every school should seek to appoint a designated senior lead for mental health. The DfE has been running funded training courses for this role since October 2021 to support staff in overseeing the strategy for a whole-school approach to mental health and wellbeing. It was proposed that all schools should have a designated senior lead for mental health by 2025. As of the end of March 2024, 70 percent of eligible schools had claimed the grant (DfE, 2024b). Those members of staff who applied for the training during the academic year 2021/22 were also asked to complete a follow-up survey. In primary schools, the data suggests that it is primarily SENCos who have taken on the role, and in secondary schools, it is most commonly the designated safeguarding lead. With these roles being all-consuming in their own right, it is no surprise that 47 percent of respondents did not feel they had enough time for the role (DfE, 2024b).

The 2017 Green Paper detailed that the designated lead is responsible for the whole school-approach to mental health and should:

- oversee the help the school gives to pupils with mental health issues

- help staff to spot pupils who show signs of poor mental health

- offer advice to staff about mental health

- refer children to specialist services if they need to.

REFLECTION POINT

What role do you play in supporting mental health in your school?

The role of all school staff in supporting mental health

This is not an exhaustive list, but there are some specific ways in which other members of school staff may support children and young people with their mental health and wellbeing. These are:

- helping children to feel safe and contained within the school context

- being emotionally available

- supporting the child or young person in identifying their relationships, resources and coping mechanisms

- maintaining appropriate boundaries, encouraging independence and supporting resilience

- being equipped with the skills and knowledge to recognize signs and symptoms of possible mental health issues in children and young people

- responding quickly, safely and appropriately to the signs of mental distress and to seek the appropriate support

- feeling confident in having safe conversations with children and young people about their mental health

- promoting mental wellbeing in the school setting, and setting a good example to others by prioritizing self-care

- promoting open dialogue around mental health within the setting to reduce the stigma around talking about mental health

- understanding the importance of mental health for learning

- taking a relational approach to supporting behaviour and understanding all behaviour as a form of communication.

Crucially, the role *does not* involve being a therapist or diagnosing mental health issues in children and young people.

I have been a teacher for 10 years and we have seen a huge rise in mental health issues in our school. It's usually our senior leadership team who get to go on Mental Health First Aid training, so I felt really out of my depth when a child in my class confided in me that he was self-harming. I didn't know what to say at first, so I just listened, and I guess that's probably right, but I don't know. I just didn't want to say the wrong thing and make things worse. (Nazeen, teacher)

Using this handbook

This handbook is specifically designed to support school staff in developing the knowledge and skills to support children and young people who display signs of poor mental health, or who have experienced heightened levels of stress and trauma. The information and resources aim to equip educators to feel empowered to respond safely and effectively to pupils in distress. All of the tools and strategies are evidence-based but can be used by anyone working in the school setting who would like to interact in a more nurturing and therapeutic way. The handbook aims to reflect the most recent research and thinking around specific mental health issues such as anxiety, emotionally based school avoidance, eating disorders and self-harm, to provide staff with the confidence they need to support the children and young people that they work with.

The first three chapters introduce the role of school staff in supporting mental health and some helpful guidance on a general approach to supporting the mental health needs in children and young people. You may choose to read the Introduction and Chapters 1, 2 and 3, and then dip into those that you require as and when the situations present themselves. It is essential to read Chapter 1 as this introduces our FIRES Framework, which we will refer to throughout the handbook.

As well as providing essential information and strategies, the chapters all include case studies, reflection points, top tips, and quotes, encouraging you to interact with the resource and bring it to life with your own experiences.

All resources in the Appendices marked with a ✳ can be downloaded as PDFs from https://library.jkp.com/redeem using the code QYEGULY. Resources in Chapters 2, 6, 7, 10, 11, 12, 14 and 15 marked with a ✳ can be photocopied freely. All downloadable and photocopiable resources can be used as many times as you like.

A final note

Ultimately, it is hoped that this resource will empower school staff to feel confident in supporting children and young people with their mental health and wellbeing. We strongly believe that those currently working in our education system have a vital, rewarding and challenging role. In amongst all their other duties, school staff are often chosen by children and young people to confide in, and be nurtured by, but may also receive very little training to allow them to feel confident in doing so.

To all those working tirelessly in our schools – we see you, and this resource is for you.

References

Barrett, P.M. & Turner, C.M. (2001) 'Prevention of anxiety symptoms in primary school children: Preliminary results from a universal school-based trial.' *British Journal of Clinical Psychology, 40*(4), 399–410.

Becerra-Culqui, T.A., Liu, Y., Nash, R., Cromwell, L. et al. (2018) 'Mental health of transgender and gender nonconforming youth compared with their peers.' *Pediatrics, 141*(5), e20173845. doi:10.1542/peds.2017-3845

Burke, N.J., Hellman, J.L., Scott, B.G., Weems, C.F. & Carrion, V.G. (2011) 'The impact of adverse childhood experiences on an urban pediatric population.' *Child Abuse and Neglect, 35*(6), 408–413.

Cecil, C.A., Viding, E., Fearon, P., Glaser, D. & McCrory, E.J. (2017) 'Disentangling the mental health impact of childhood abuse and neglect.' *Child Abuse and Neglect, 63*(1), 106–119.

Centre for Mental Health (2016) *Missed Opportunities: A Review of Recent Evidence into Children and Young People's Mental Health.* www.centreformentalhealth.org.uk/wp-content/uploads/2018/09/CentreforMentalHealth_MissedOpportunities.pdf

Chakraborty, A., McManus, S., Brugha, T.S., Bebbington, P. & King, M. (2011) 'Mental health of the non-heterosexual population of England.' *British Journal of Psychiatry, 198*, 143–148.

Chida, Y, Steptoe, A. (2008) 'Positive psychological wellbeing and mortality: A quantitative review of prospective observational studies.' *Psychosomatic Medicine, 70*, 741–756.

Children's Commissioner (2021) Annual report 2020–21. www.childrenscommissioner.gov.uk/about-us/corporate-governance/annual-report-2020-21

Deacon, B.J., Lickel, J.J., Farrell, N.R., Kemp, J.J. & Hipol, L.J. (2013) 'Therapist perceptions and delivery of interoceptive exposure for panic disorder.' *Journal of Anxiety Disorders, 27*, 259–264.

Department for Education (2014) *Keeping Children Safe in Education: Information for All School and College Staff.* www.rbkc.gov.uk/pdf/DfE%20Keeping%20Children%20Safe%20in%20Education%202014%20-%20SUMMARY.pdf

Department for Education (2018) *Promoting Children and Young People's Mental Health and Wellbeing: A Whole School or College Approach.* https://assets.publishing.service.gov.uk/media/614cc965d3bf7f718518029c/Promoting_children_and_young_people_s_mental_health_and_wellbeing.pdf

Department for Education (2024a) *Keeping Children Safe in Education 2024: Statutory Guidance for Schools and Colleges on Safeguarding Children and Safer Recruitment.* www.gov.uk/government/publications/keeping-children-safe-in-education--2

Department for Education (2024b) *Transforming Children and Young People's Mental Health Implementation Programme: Data Release.* https://assets.publishing.service.gov.uk/media/6641f1e1ae748c43d37939a3/Transforming_children_and_young_people_s_mental_health_implementation_programme_2024_data_release.pdf

Department of Health & Department for Education (2017) *Transforming Children and Young People's Mental Health Provision: A Green Paper* https://assets.publishing.

service.gov.uk/government/uploads/system/uploads/attachment_data/file/664855/
Transforming_children_and_young_people_s_mental_health_provision.pdf

Early Intervention Foundation (2022) 'Every interaction is an intervention': How our new practical guide can support teachers to support students' mental health. www.eif.org.uk/blog/every-interaction-is-an-intervention-how-our-new-practical-guide-can-support-teachers-to-support-students-mental-health

Education Executive (2018, 11 April) NEU survey reveals the impact of school pressures on student mental health. https://edexec.co.uk/neu-survey-reveals-the-impact-of-school-pressures-on-student-mental-health

Faulconbridge, J., Hunt, K. & Laffan, A. (2019) *Improving the Psychological Wellbeing of Children and Young People: Effective Prevention and Early Intervention Across Health, Education and Social Care.* London: Jessica Kingsley Publishers.

Fonagy, P. (2019) When adversity turns into trauma: Understanding the long term effects of adverse childhood experience [Slide presentation]. www.transformationpartners.nhs.uk/wp-content/uploads/2019/07/Peter-Fonagy-When-adversity-turns-into-trauma.pdf

Gavin, H. (2011) 'Sticks and stones may break my bones: The effects of emotional abuse.' *Journal of Aggression, Maltreatment and Trauma, 20*(5), 503–529.

Gutman, L.M. & Vorhaus, J. (2012) *The Impact of Pupil Behaviour and Wellbeing on Educational Outcomes.* https://assets.publishing.service.gov.uk/media/5a747ef34 0fob604dd7ae609/DFE-RR253.pdf

Haidt, J. (2024) *The Anxious Generation: How the Great Rewiring of Childhood Is Causing an Epidemic of Mental Illness.* New York, NY: Penguin.

Kabat-Zinn, J. (2005) *Wherever You Go, There You Are: Mindfulness Meditation in Everyday Life.* New York, NY: Hyperion.

Kessler, R.C., Berglund, P., Demler, O., Jin, R., Merikangas, K.R. & Walters, E.E. (2005) 'Lifetime prevalence and age-of-onset distributions of DSM-IV disorders in the National Comorbidity Survey Replication.' *Archives of General Psychiatry, 62*(6), 593–602.

Lewis, S.J., Arseneault, L., Caspi, A., Fisher, H.L. et al. (2019) 'The epidemiology of trauma and post-traumatic stress disorder in a representative cohort of young people in England and Wales.' *Lancet Psychiatry, 6*(3), 247–256.

Mind (2020) Mental health problems – an introduction. www.mind.org.uk/information-support/types-of-mental-health-problems/mental-health-problems-introduction/about-mental-health-problems

NASUWT (2024) The Big Question Report 2023. www.nasuwt.org.uk/news/campaigns/big-question-survey.html

National Youth Advocacy Service (2019) *Looked After Minds: Prioritising the Mental Health of Care-Experienced Children and Young People.* London: National Youth Advocacy Service.

NHS (2020) Mental Health of Children and Young People in England, 2020. https://digital.nhs.uk/data-and-information/publications/statistical/mental-health-of-children-and-young-people-in-england/2020-wave-1-follow-up

NHS (2023) Mental Health of Children and Young People in England, 2022. https://digital.nhs.uk/data-and-information/publications/statistical/mental-health-of-children-and-young-people-in-england/2023-wave-4-follow-up

Norman, R.E., Byambaa, M. De, R., Butchart, A., Scott, J. & Vos, T. (2012) 'The long-term health consequences of child physical abuse, emotional abuse, and neglect: A systematic review and meta-analysis.' *PLoS Med, 9*(11), e1001349. doi:10.1371/journal.pmed.1001349

NSPCC (2019) *Childline Annual Review 2018/19.* London: NSPCC.

Ofsted (2023) Education inspection framework. www.gov.uk/government/publications/education-inspection-framework/education-inspection-framework-for-september-2023

Pressman, S.D. & Cohen, S. (2005) 'Does positive affect influence health?' *Psychological Bulletin, 131*, 925–971.

Race Equality Foundation (2020) *Racial Disparities in Mental Health: Literature and Evidence Review*. London: Race Equality Foundation.

Schaefer, J.D., Caspi, A., Belsky, D.W., Harrington, H. et al. (2017) 'Enduring mental health: Prevalence and prediction.' *Journal of Abnormal Psychology, 126*(2), 212–224, doi:10.1037/abn0000232

Sunderland, M. (2022) *Helping Children and Teenagers Talk About Their Lives Using the Arts and the Danger of Un-storied Emotions* [Video] www.childmentalhealthcentre.org/webinars/webinars-single-viewers/product/111-helping-children-and-young-people-talk-about-their-lives-using-arts-and-the-danger-of-un-storied-emotions

Treisman, K. (2017) *Working with Relational and Developmental Trauma in Children and Adolescents*. London: Routledge.

Weare, K. (2000) *Promoting Mental, Emotional and Social Health: A Whole School Approach*. London: Routledge.

Widom, C.S. (1999) 'Posttraumatic stress disorder in abused and neglected children grown up.' *American Journal of Psychiatry, 156*(8), 1223–1229.

World Health Organization (2024) Mental Health. www.who.int/health-topics/mental-health#tab=tab_1

CHAPTER 1

Understanding Mental Health and the FIRES Framework

What is mental health?

Mental health includes our emotional, social and psychological wellbeing. It impacts how we think, feel and behave. It also determines how we cope with the ups and downs of daily life, and how we interact others. Mental health is important throughout the entire lifespan.

When we experience difficulties with our mental health, our thoughts, emotions and behaviours can all be affected. There are many factors that can contribute to mental health issues, such as:

- biological factors (e.g. genes, brain structure or biochemistry)

- adverse life experiences, such as bereavement, abuse or bullying

- family history of mental health difficulties.

It is important to note that feeling sad, anxious or angry are normal emotional states that we all experience. Not only are they normal, but they are also useful to us. In very simple terms, anxiety helps to keep us safe by making us vigilant to threats around us, sadness attracts connection from those around us when we most need support, and anger motivates us to act when we feel that we have been wronged. We need those emotions! However, normal emotions can become signs of a mental health issue when they are causing significant distress over a prolonged period and impairing our ability to function.

Early warning signs of problems

Mental health issues have many different signs and symptoms, but some common signs of a mental health need could be:

- eating too much or too little
- sleeping too much or too little
- isolating oneself from people
- withdrawing from usual activities
- having little or no energy
- feeling constantly tired
- feeling numb, apathetic or like nothing matters
- feelings of hopelessness
- increase in smoking, drinking or drug-taking
- changes in usual behaviour
- feeling more confused, angry, upset or on edge
- being irritable and agitated
- experiencing mood swings so severe that they cause problems in relationships
- having persistent intrusive thoughts or flashbacks
- hallucinations or delusions
- thoughts of harming yourself or someone else
- thoughts about ending your own life
- inability to function adequately due to your emotional state.

Conversely, *positive mental health* allows people to:

- fulfil their potential
- respond with resilience in the face of adversity
- be productive and fruitful
- find meaning and purpose in their lives.

Ways to *maintain* positive mental health include:

- seeking professional help when needed
- practising gratitude, positivity and kindness
- connecting with other people
- spending time in nature
- exercise
- getting enough sleep
- having a healthy diet.

'I used to think self-care was just about exercise and healthy eating, but I've learned that what I really need is a bit of quiet time each day to myself to relax and unwind after a busy day at school. I used to feel guilty, but I know I can't look after others if I don't put on my oxygen mask first.' (Tracey, SENCo)

Children and young people

Poor emotional and mental health affects a significant number of children and young people:

- In 2023, one in five children (aged 8–25 years) had a probable mental health disorder; around six pupils in every classroom (NHS, 2023).
- Half of all mental health problems are established by the age of 14, with 75 percent by age 24 (Kessler et al., 2005).

A substantial body of research evidence (e.g. Kim, Allen & Jimerson, 2024) suggests that young people's social, emotional and mental health (SEMH) needs have a significant impact on all aspects of their lives, including their learning and progress through the curriculum, behaviour and attendance at school, further training and employment, and general life chances.

There is a growing understanding and recognition within society that mental health is more than the absence of mental illness. *Good mental health needs to be protected, nurtured and promoted.*

It is also important that we all continue to challenge some of the myths and stigmas surrounding mental health. Take a look at the statements about mental health in Table 1.1 to see which are myths and which are reality.

Table 1.1 Mental health myths and reality

Statement	Myth or Reality	Explanation	
Mental health issues are rare.	MYTH	Mental health issues affect one in four people every year (Public Health England, 2019). So even if you don't have a mental health problem, it's likely your best friend, a family member or work colleague will be affected.	
People with mental health issues are often violent.	MYTH	People with mental health issues are much more likely to be the victims of violence (Khalifeh et al., 2015). This myth makes it more difficult for people to talk openly about mental health issues. It can also lead to the loss of friendships and relationships at the time that they are needed most.	
People can't work if they have a mental health issue.	MYTH	With one in four people affected, you probably work with someone with a mental health issue.	
People with mental health problems never recover.	MYTH	Many people can and do recover completely from mental health issues. Alongside professional help, the support of friends, family and getting back to work are all important in helping people recover.	
Other people can't tell if you have a mental health problem.	REALITY	Mental health problems are as real as, for example, a broken arm – although there isn't a sling or plaster cast to show for it. Many of those who are affected deal with it alone because nobody else knows.	
We all have mental health, just as we all have physical health.	REALITY	In the same way that we wouldn't expect always to be physically healthy, our mental health will also vary from time to time, and it is important that we take care of both. We should treat our mental health like we do our dental health.	
Mental health issues are on the rise.	REALITY	In 2017, it was estimated that one in nine children between the ages of 5 and 16 had a diagnosable mental health issue. In 2023, it had increased to one in five (NHS, 2023).	

REFLECTION POINT

Stop to think about these myths and consider your responses here. How do you think of mental health? Do you recognize/have you experienced some difficulties or the stigma which still exists around this whole topic? How do you think your lived experience might inform the way you support children and young people in school?

Understanding school-based systems and support, and where you fit in

In any school-based context, there will be a range of support systems and mechanisms to identify children and young people at risk of developing mental health problems. There will also, hopefully, be a range of initiatives and interventions designed to support those at risk, and also those displaying difficulties such as anxiety, depression, emotionally based school avoidance, as well as learning, sensory and behavioural needs.

What is important is that you understand what your role is in terms of providing support, and also how you can be nurtured and supported yourself to be able to take on such a role effectively and safely.

What you need to know

The senior mental health lead in school is responsible for overseeing the identification of mental health difficulties and coordinating intervention, including making referrals for specialist support. Thus, senior mental health leads in schools will be involved in 'supporting the identification of at-risk children and children exhibiting signs of mental ill health' (DoH & DfE, 2017). They will also be a pathway to specialist support: 'For those children and young people who develop a mental health problem, we are committed to increasing the support available as quickly as possible' (DoH & DfE, 2017).

The DfE's 2018 document *Mental Health and Behaviour in Schools* specified two routes to identifying mental health difficulties:

- 'effective use of data so that changes in pupils' patterns of attainment, attendance or behaviour are noticed and can be acted on; along with

- an effective pastoral system so that at least one member of staff (e.g. a form tutor or class teacher) knows every pupil well and has received training to spot where changes in behaviour may have a root cause that needs addressing. Where this is the case, the mental health lead, pastoral system (including school nurses) or school policies should provide the structure through which staff can escalate the issue and make decisions about what to do next. This system should also provide the opportunity for pupils to seek support confidentially.'

So, it is highly likely that in your role supporting children and young people with social, emotional and mental health needs, you may well receive training and ongoing support and direction from the designated senior mental health lead in your school.

It is vital, therefore, at the outset, that you are very clear about your responsibilities and any routes for raising concerns about individual children or young people.

'I worry that I'll say or do the wrong thing and make things worse. It feels like a big responsibility and, if anything bad happened because I didn't do the right thing, I'd never forgive myself.' (Rebecca, teaching assistant)

Within your school, it is important to be clear on the safeguarding procedures around mental health concerns, including:

- how you raise any concerns with your mental health lead or designated safeguarding lead

- when a mental health concern is also a safeguarding concern

- the process for making records of your concerns

- what to do in any medical emergency, when the child or young person presents as at risk, or is clearly engaging in self-harming behaviours

- how to make the right decision regarding confidentiality and the fact that any information shared with you by a child or young person can never be considered entirely confidential

- how, when and why you might need to involve the parents or caregivers of a child or young person.

Top tips and strategies
Starting with you

An important point that needs to be raised at the outset is the fact that when you are taking on a role that involves identifying and supporting children and young people with a range of wellbeing issues or mental health needs, then you must initially make sure that you also look after yourself and your own needs. Discussions around self-care often focus upon eating well and making time for exercise. However, 'wellbeing' refers to so much more than just physical wellbeing, also encompassing emotional, spiritual and mental wellness (see Figure 1.1).

FIGURE 1.1 AREAS OF WELLBEING

REFLECTION POINT

Stop and think about what you are currently doing to maintain your own wellbeing. Think about the four key areas of wellbeing: spiritual, emotional, physical and mental. Take a look at the chart below and try to identify at least one thing that you are currently doing to maintain your overall wellbeing. We will return to this again in subsequent chapters, as this is something that will need a continual focus to avoid it falling down the list of priorities amongst all of your other responsibilities.

Recognizing issues in children and young people

Everyone in the school community needs to be able to recognize the signs that a child may be struggling. However, *it is important to remember that some mental health issues may not have visible signs.* There are also factors that might make it more difficult for a child or young person to ask for help.

Some children and young people may try to hide how they are feeling or what they are doing (Theodosiou et al., 2020). The Mental Health Foundation and Camelot Foundation (2006) suggested that this might be because they:

- worry they won't be taken seriously

- believe others won't understand

- have had a negative experience talking about their thoughts and feelings in the past

- feel that no one can help them

- fear being dismissed or labelled an attention seeker or 'crazy'.

'I didn't want anyone to know that I'd been self-harming. I thought they'd just think I was doing it for attention. It was totally the opposite from that; I didn't want any attention at all; I just wanted everyone to leave me alone.' (Brandon, 17)

Children and young people may not always have the language or ability to communicate their feelings. They may be unsure who to talk to and how to discuss their problems. Some signs of mental health issues may also look like normal age-appropriate behaviour, for example, tantrums in younger children, or teenagers keeping feelings to themselves.

Children who have experienced abuse may be reluctant to talk about how they are feeling, particularly if they haven't yet told anyone about the abuse. They may feel that something is wrong with them or that things may get worse if they talk about it. Identifying and responding to mental health concerns may be one way of helping children who are experiencing abuse get the support and protection that they need.

Signs of child mental health issues

There are ways you can identify if a child needs support with their mental health. You can recognize patterns that suggest they need support by being attentive to a child or young person's mood and behaviour. Common warning signs of mental health issues include:

- sudden mood and behaviour changes

- self-harming

- unexplained physical changes, such as weight gain or weight loss

- sudden poor academic behaviour or performance

- sleeping problems

- changes in social habits, such as withdrawing or avoiding friends and family.

These signs suggest that a child may be struggling, but there could be several different explanations for them. *Do not attempt to diagnose mental health issues yourself or make assumptions about what is happening in a child's life.* Recognizing that a child or young person may be struggling with their mental health is the first step in helping them. The next step is to respond appropriately.

A clear pathway

Look at Figure 1.2 overleaf, which gives you a clear pathway in terms of where to go when you are concerned about a pupil's mental health. It is very important that you discuss this with the management team, senior mental health lead (MHL) and designated safeguarding lead (DSL), to ensure that the pathway fits with current policy and practice in your school. However, the steps shown here are regarded as best practice in order to maintain a safe and ethical approach. A full-page downloadable version of this flowchart can be found in the Appendices.

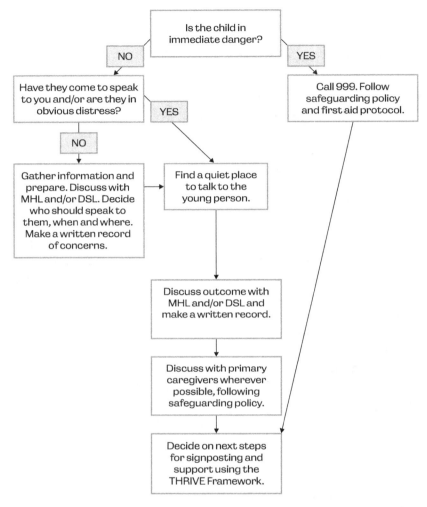

FIGURE 1.2 MENTAL HEALTH RESPONSE FLOWCHART

CASE STUDY

Raoul is a PE teacher in a secondary school. He has noticed that Sarah, a student in Year 8, has been behaving differently recently. She has become more withdrawn and is isolating herself from her friends. Sarah used to love PE, but now avoids taking part. Raoul noticed that despite the warm July weather, Sarah never took off her blazer. One of her friends confided in Raoul that they are concerned that she might be self-harming again. Spurred on by this, Raoul knew to act fast and decided to confront Sarah, asking her if she is harming herself and encouraging her to show him her arms. Sarah started to cry and ran away. She didn't attend school yesterday and now Raoul is doubting whether he did the right thing.

Questions

1. What warning signs were there that may alert you to thinking that Sarah might be self-harming?

2. What would you have done in this situation?

3. Was Raoul right to act quickly and confront Sarah?

Raoul was right to act quickly and not ignore the warning signs (i.e. change in behaviour, staying covered up, withdrawing, concerns from peers, past self-harming). However, acting quickly does not necessarily mean leaping in to confront the young person immediately, without preparing for the conversation, if they are not in immediate danger or obvious distress. In this situation, Sarah had already confided in her head of year, and the issue was known to the mental health lead and designated safeguarding lead, who were coordinating the support for Sarah. Sarah had been referred to the Child and Adolescent Mental Health Service (CAMHS) and was receiving support in school. But she was embarrassed about her self-harming and eager for no one else to know. Having another member of staff confront her about this, out of the blue, left her feeling mortified and ashamed.

If the young person is not in immediate distress or danger, and has not approached you to discuss the issue, it is wise to act quickly by informing the mental health lead and designated safeguarding lead about your concerns. A written record of these concerns should be made, and an agreement reached about appropriate next steps. In this case, such a conversation would have meant that Raoul would have had his concerns validated, and he would have been reassured that appropriate measures had already been taken to support Sarah. Raoul also made the mistake of focusing on Sarah's injuries, rather than on her emotional distress. If he had made her emotional wellbeing the primary focus of his conversation with Sarah, the discussion may have felt more supportive.

The FIRES Framework

Ideally, most of the time, schools will be working with mental health at a preventative level rather than being reactive and 'firefighting'; but, in situations where children are struggling to cope with their mental health, there will be fires to be fought. To give you a memorable, effective and safe response when supporting a child with a mental health need, we have developed a framework for action with the acronym FIRES (developed by Ali D'Amario, first published in Rae, 2023) (Figure 1.3).

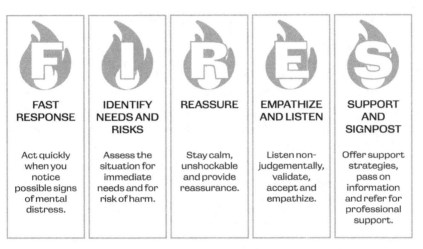

FIGURE 1.3 THE FIRES FRAMEWORK (REPRODUCED BY PERMISSION OF TAYLOR & FRANCIS GROUP)

Fast response

Act quickly when you notice possible signs of mental distress:

- Don't ignore it – act as soon as possible when you suspect that a child may be experiencing distress. Remember that it is always better to raise the issue and be wrong than not to raise it and be right.

- Where possible, the first port-of-call should be to speak to the mental health lead or safeguarding lead and work together to create an appropriate plan.

- Prepare yourself emotionally for the conversation and make sure that you have the information needed to be able to respond effectively.

- Whilst it is important to act quickly, you must also make sure that you have appropriate time and space for the conversation with the young person. If a young person approaches you wanting to talk and you are unable to, options could be to ask someone to cover your class if possible, find someone else that the young person would be able to speak to or set aside a time later that day to talk to the young person and reassure them that the conversation is important to you.

- Get down to their level to help them to feel at ease.

- Consider whether you need to make use of eye contact to show that you are listening, or whether this might increase the child's level of anxiety and prevent a more authentic dialogue. Alternatives could be doing an activity together whilst talking or walking side-by-side.

- Let the pupil know that you are there to talk to them if they'd like to talk to you, but do not push them to open up if they're not ready to do so. If they do not want to talk initially, ensure that you check in regularly. Find out if there is anyone that they have spoken to or could speak to. If not, you may like to let them know that they can talk confidentially to Childline. This can be a helpful step in opening communication and will avoid a young person suffering in silence. It may also then give them the confidence to talk to you or to seek support from someone else around them.

- Make sure that you establish expectations around confidentiality. It is important to tell them at the outset that you cannot keep secrets and may have to pass the information on in order to keep them safe and get them the help that they need.

Identify needs and risks

Assess the situation for immediate needs and for risk of harm:

- Ask yourself if there are any immediate risks – is a young person at risk to themselves or others at this time?

- Is there a risk that the young person may be feeling suicidal? The only way to really know this is to ask them. This can feel daunting, but research shows that connecting and opening this dialogue puts the child at less risk than if they are having these thoughts and don't feel like they can share it. Phrases to use might include. 'Have you been having thoughts about ending your life?' See Chapter 13 for more guidance on talking about suicide safely.

- Is there any way in which the child or young person could harm themselves?

- Could there be a medical emergency (e.g. cuts, overdose, asthma attack, etc.)?

- Are alcohol or drugs present? These both increase the risk of self-harm and suicide and should be removed as soon as possible.

- Does the child or young person need space, or do they need closeness?

- Who would be the best person to help in this particular situation? Generally, it will be the person that the child has a relationship with and trusts. This is why it is so important that all school staff have training and confidence in this area.

- Is this environment right for them at this point in time? Can they be moved? Where are they most likely to feel safe?

Reassure
Stay calm, unshockable and provide reassurance:

- This is not about promising the child that everything will be okay, but you can reassure the child or young person that you are there to help them to get the support they need, and that they are not alone.

- Normalize their emotions, but be careful not to belittle their feelings.

- Be sure to take what they are saying seriously, even if it feels trivial or irrational to you.

- Be unshockable and non-judgemental. It will have taken the child or young person a lot of courage to share their feelings with you, and they need to feel that their frightening emotions are not frightening for you. This will help them to feel that you can contain their emotions for them and relieve some of the distress that they are experiencing.

Empathize and listen

Listen non-judgementally, validate, accept and empathize:

- Empathy means taking the perspective of another person and surrendering your own opinions in order to understand someone else. This creates a safe space where pupils feel comfortable being themselves and sharing their concerns.

- Make use of open questions to encourage the child or young person to communicate and talk to you.

- Use reflective listening to show the child or young person that you are listening and understanding them. It may be helpful to reflect back to them any feelings that you can sense, for example, 'It sounds like you're feeling really overwhelmed.'

- Offer empathy and understanding rather than solutions. If the solution was that easy, there wouldn't be a problem. Trying to fix it will mean that you are busy thinking about what to say, rather than really hearing them. This will result in them feeling disempowered and that you haven't really understood.

- Every time that you get tempted to give advice, ask an open question instead.

- Always be patient, warm and friendly, and give your full attention to the child or young person.

- To really allow you to feel free to listen rather than give advice, it may help to have a stock phrase to say after they have had chance to fully express how they are feeling. For example, 'I'm really sorry that you're feeling this way, but I am so glad that you told me.'

Support and signpost

Offer support strategies, pass on information and refer for professional support:

- Keep the solutions child-centred. Most of the time we have the answers to our own problems; we just need someone else to help us find them. Rather than giving your ideas, try to ask them questions, such as 'What could I do to help?', 'What could your parents do that would help?', 'Is there anything that you could do that would make this better?' or 'What would be one small step that we could take that would make a difference to you today?'

- Check with the child whether there is anyone else that they have talked to or could talk to.

- Try to establish protective factors that support their resilience (e.g. positive relationships with friends or family, interests and hobbies).

- Signpost to other sources of information or support. You may find it helpful to use the THRIVE Framework described in the next section.

- Be clear what you will do with the information that they have told you and who it will be shared with. Information should always be shared with the mental health lead and designated safeguarding lead. Parents and carers should be informed in most situations, unless it is assessed as putting the child at more risk. See your school safeguarding policy for further guidance.

It is crucial that the 'S' part of the FIRES Framework comes at the end. Not only because the acronym would fall apart with it anywhere else, but also because you need to do all of the other steps before you start to offer advice. As Gottman & DeClaire (1997) state, 'To propose solutions before you empathize with children is like trying to build the frame of a house before you lay a firm foundation.' (p.120).

The FIRES Framework can be used in this form for responding to any mental health need and will help to guide you through the process safely. However, there are some specific things to consider at each stage for different mental health issues, and therefore we will return to the FIRES Framework throughout the handbook, with additional considerations to think about for each stage. There is also a downloadable full-page FIRES poster in the Appendices for you to display in your school.

THRIVE Framework

The THRIVE Framework (Wolpert et al., 2019) is a useful tool to use when thinking about the signposting and support that a young person may need. It is an approach to delivering mental health services for children, young people and their families that was developed by professionals from the Tavistock and Portman NHS Foundation Trust and the Anna Freud National Centre for Children and Families.

The framework aims to provide a shared language for school staff and mental health services to use when considering the level of support required by a child or young person. This means that the help provided is not based on diagnosis, rather the framework can help schools in reflecting on the preventative support in place for children who are 'thriving', what signposting and advice they can give to those in need of early intervention, and ensuring that targeted support is available within schools to support those experiencing greater challenges with their mental health. Through thinking about needs in this way, together with families, it may be that a child's mental health needs can be supported in school, or through local charities and organizations, rather than always requiring a referral to CAMHS.

The THRIVE Framework divides support into five areas:

- thriving – universal strategies to support positive mental health

- getting advice – for young people whose needs can be met through providing some advice or signposting to support

- getting help – for students who need targeted support to promote wellbeing

- getting more help – more specialist mental health support

- getting risk support – for children and young people at high risk who cannot access support or for pupils who are considered to experience significant mental health needs despite support.

Some examples of interventions and support strategies that could be offered under these five categories are shown in Table 1.2. It can be very useful to reflect upon what provision you have available within school and in your local area, and to identify any gaps and areas for development.

Table 1.2 Interventions and support strategies

Thriving	Getting advice	Getting help	Getting more help	Getting risk support
PSHE programmes Whole-school approach to mental health Supporting resilience of vulnerable group Monitoring wellbeing Staff training Supporting parents Promoting a culture of wellbeing	Workshops Apps Mentors Wellbeing ambassadors	Primary mental health workers ELSA support Rainbows bereavement groups Educational psychologist Nurture groups School counsellor Drawing and talking therapy Education mental health practitioner	CAMHS Other mental health specialists providing ongoing support	Multi-agency support around the child and family Children's services

Monitoring pupil wellbeing/mental health

Just as attendance and attainment are closely monitored by schools, it is also important to measure and record pupil wellbeing. Using surveys to assess staff and pupil wellbeing can be invaluable for several reasons:

- They provide an overall snapshot of how the children and young people are feeling in your school.

- They allow schools to measure the impact of support that is put in place for individual interventions, group interventions or whole-school approaches.

- Crucially, they will allow for the identification and support of pupils who may otherwise have suffered in silence and flown beneath the radar.

School staff will need to think carefully about how this monitoring could be done within their context. There are some online companies (e.g. Bounce Together) that allow for students to be screened using standardized measures at the press of button. As questionnaires are completed, the software performs analyses and makes comparisons. Predictably, these software packages tend to be very expensive, but they are time-efficient. Without this software, screening may involve the use of assessment tools, such as:

- standardized questionnaires (e.g. the Boxall Profile: Bennathan, 1998; Strengths & Difficulties Questionnaire (SDQ): Goodman, 1997)

- a self-report questionnaire or simple scale developed in school (see example below).

Alternatives to screening as a method of identifying possible difficulties include:

- carefully monitoring data already collected in school, including attendance, punctuality, achievement and behaviour reports

- parental concerns forms

- staff concerns forms

- collecting regular feedback from staff on student wellbeing

- opportunities for students to self-refer.

If you do decide to create your own survey with children and young people, it can be helpful to make use of the following simple format.

Possible survey questions for children and young people
Please rate each of the following statements from 1 to 10 (1 = very strongly disagree, 10 = very strongly agree).

1. At my school, teachers care about pupils/students.

2. I feel safe at school.

3. School is fun.

4. Adults at my school treat pupils/students fairly.

5. People at school notice when I am good at something.

6. I can be myself at school.

7. This is a friendly school.

8. I am happy to be at this school.

9. There is something for everyone to enjoy at school.

10. I find school interesting.

11. The school takes bullying seriously.

12. Bullying is usually dealt with well.

13. People help me when I find my work difficult.

14. I know how to get help when I am stuck with work.

15. The school values my opinions.

16. I know how to get my views listened to at school.

17. I have someone to talk to if I have a problem.

18. I usually have something to do at break time.

19. I usually have something to do at lunchtime.

20. I am happy to use the toilets when I need to.

21. I feel good about school life.

22. Lessons usually interest me.

23. I know what my learning style is.

24. There is someone I can talk to at school if I have worries.

25. There is an adult I can talk to in school if I have worries.

26. The school has fair values.

27. Children are treated fairly at school.

28. School helps me to learn about the people in my community.

29. School helps me learn about clubs or activities in my community.

Clearly, this chapter is not aimed at providing you with an in-depth understanding of mental health and, specifically, the mental health difficulties or wellbeing issues that young people encounter in today's complex world. However, we do provide additional information and support in the subsequent chapters, to develop your knowledge base and skills in a range of key areas, thus increasing your confidence in taking on the role of supporting the mental health needs of children and young people.

References

Bennathan M. (1998) *The Boxall Profile: Handbook for Teachers*. Maidstone: AWCEBD.

Department for Education (2018) *Mental Health and Behaviour in Schools*. https://assets.publishing.service.gov.uk/media/625ee6148fa8f54a8bb65ba9/Mental_health_and_behaviour_in_schools.pdf

Department of Health & Department for Education (2017) *Transforming Children and Young People's Mental Health Provision: A Green Paper* https://assets.publishing.service.gov.uk/government/uploads/system/uploads/attachment_data/file/664855/Transforming_children_and_young_people_s_mental_health_provision.pdf

Goodman, R. (1997) 'The Strengths and Difficulties Questionnaire: A research note.' *Journal of Child Psychology & Psychiatry 38*(5), 581–586.

Gottman, J. & DeClaire, J. (1997) *Raising an Emotionally Intelligent Child*. Hoboken, NJ: Prentice Hall.

Kessler, R.C., Berglund, P., Demler, O., Jin, R., Merikangas, K.R. & Walters, E.E. (2005) 'Lifetime prevalence and age-of-onset distributions of DSM-IV disorders in the National Comorbidity Survey Replication.' *Archives of General Psychiatry, 62*(6), 593–602.

Khalifeh, H., Johnson, S., Howard, L.M., Borschmann, R. et al. (2015) 'Violent and non-violent crime against adults with severe mental illness.' *British Journal of Psychiatry, 206*(4), 275–282.

Kim, E.K., Allen, J.P. & Jimerson, S.R. (2024) 'Supporting student social emotional learning and development.' *School Psychology Review, 53*(3), 201–207.

NHS (2023) Mental Health of Children and Young People in England, 2022. https://digital.nhs.uk/data-and-information/publications/statistical/mental-health-of-children-and-young-people-in-england/2023-wave-4-follow-up

Mental Health Foundation and Camelot Foundation (2006) *Truth Hurts: Report on the National Inquiry into Self-harm Among Young People*. London: Mental Health Foundation.

Public Health England (2019) Health profile for England: 2019. www.gov.uk/government/publications/health-profile-for-england-2019

Rae, T. (2023) *Understanding and Supporting Refugee Children and Young People: A Practical Resource for Teachers, Parents and Carers of Those Exposed to the Trauma of War*. London: David Fulton.

Theodosiou L., Knightsmith, P., Lavis, P. & Bailey, S. (2020) *Children and Young People's Mental Health: Early Intervention, Ongoing Support and Flexible Evidence-based Care*. Shoreham-by-Sea: Pavilion.

Wolpert, M., Harris, R., Hodges, S., Fuggle, P. et al. (2019) *THRIVE Framework for System Change*. London: CAMHS Press.

CHAPTER 2

Understanding Your Role in Supporting Mental Health and Reflective Practice

This handbook has started by presenting you with a general overview of the role of the school staff in supporting the mental health of children and young people. It has also highlighted that there is now a greater emphasis on promoting wellbeing and supporting the mental health and wellbeing of children and young people, as opposed to just focusing on teaching and supporting their learning. In many cases, teaching assistants are becoming pivotal in delivering evidence-based pre-emptive interventions ethically and safely.

As stated previously, *supporting mental health in schools does not require you to become a therapist or to diagnose*. It is essential to continually highlight this fact. However, there is a need for school staff to have the skills and confidence to engage more therapeutically with children and young people who may well have experienced or are currently experiencing heightened levels of stress, anxiety and trauma in their lives. Being able to do this safely is essential.

When children and young people need to talk about their feelings, their emotions, their fears and anxieties, they need to do so with adults who can *truly listen*, are non-judgemental and who understand how to be regulated themselves so that they can share their skills and knowledge base, thus ensuring that young people can do likewise. Having a safe space to do this, and knowing that the adult they are talking to will indeed listen, is critical for young people who may be distressed and anxious.

For many children and teenagers, the cause of anxiety is something very frightening that happened in their lives, which left them feeling profoundly unsafe in the world. Common examples include being bullied or shamed at school, parents splitting up, a parent leaving the family home, a frightening teacher or parent, multiple school moves, or living with a parent with addiction issues. For others, the underlying feelings of fear, grief, shame, and so on, originate from living with parents who themselves are anxious.

'I used to love coming back to school after the school holidays because it was my safe place. The adults were always there, they noticed me, and I knew what to expect each day.' (Tamara, adult who witnessed domestic abuse as a child)

The emotionally available adult

Research shows that the best way to alleviate anxiety linked to trauma, as opposed to just trying to 'manage' anxiety, is to address the feelings experienced at the time of the painful life event (e.g. Amir et al., 1998). That said, it is not possible to do this alone, only in the presence of an *emotionally available adult*, one who can listen, empathize and help the child/young person to make sense of the traumatic event. This is because the feelings about the traumatic event are often deemed by the child/young person as too dangerous to feel on their own (e.g. fear of the strength of their grief, fear of shame, fear of going mad, fear of the strength of their rage), which is why anxiety developed in the first place. As Freud (1920) suggests, 'anxiety protects man from fright' (p.7, Part 3).

Children and young people need to know how unaddressed trauma can fuel anxiety because most of them have no idea. Anxious teenagers, for example, are often highly aware and eloquent about their symptoms: panic attacks, psychosomatic manifestations (after endless 'all clears' from doctors), phobias, obsessions, heart palpitations – but not about the cause of those symptoms. However, with a supportive, curious inquiry from an adult trained to listen, many will accurately and easily recall the life events that changed everything for them and left them feeling fundamentally unsafe in the world.

As Margot Sunderland (2022) states, underlying any anxiety is an impaired ability to think about feelings meaningfully. In other words, anxiety is fuelled by wordless sensations, known by some as 'unstoried emotions'. With help from a trained adult to make sense of the original trauma, the anxious child can find relief by putting painful feelings into words. Heather Geddes (2006) observed that these unbearable feelings can transform into 'thinkable thoughts', meaning that a traumatic memory can evolve from a haunting nightmare into an integrated part of a person's life story.

> *'Mrs Dunne asked me how I was each day, and I'd always say I was fine, but I think she knew I wasn't. I just didn't know how to put everything that I was feeling into words. I thought if I let my emotions out that I'd cry and never stop.' (Tamara, adult who witnessed domestic abuse as a child)*

REFLECTION POINT

Why do you want to support young people with their wellbeing? Take some time to reflect on your own experiences and what has brought you to this place. Maybe make use of a timeline, mind map or life map to reflect on your own experiences as a child and an adult and how you have managed to navigate your way through more difficult situations in your life.

Think about your own levels of resilience in your own ability to bounce back when things become difficult or very tough. Also think about what strategies you currently use in order to maintain your own wellbeing. What do you do? How do you look after yourself so that you can look after others? This might be by scheduling in regular time with loved ones, or time alone doing an activity that you really enjoy, like painting, having a bath, baking, dancing or singing. It might be making time for regular exercise or listening to your favourite playlist on your journey home. Self-care looks different for all of us, but it's important to reflect on what makes you feel really good, and to make time for it. How do you ensure that you are honest with yourself and able to reflect on your negative thinking patterns? For example, do you tend to always predict the worst? How can you feel confident that you will be able to maintain your wellbeing while supporting children and young people with difficulties of this nature?

SWOT ANALYSIS: SUPPORTING MENTAL HEALTH	
Strengths	**Weaknesses**
The strengths that you have that prepare you to support children and young people with their mental health:	Your areas for improvement in supporting young people with their mental health:
The strengths that your school has in the support being provided:	Areas for development within the school for supporting mental health:
Opportunities	**Threats**
How you might use your strengths to best effect within the school environment:	What risks there may be to you and your own wellbeing:
Opportunities available that could help you to build on your skills:	What risks there are in school that might prevent you from supporting mental health of children and young people:

REFLECTION POINT

Consider what kinds of skills you might need to develop further and how making use of this publication might help you to do exactly that. Undertaking a SWOT analysis is one way to identify: your current strengths, both internally and in your workplace, any weaknesses or areas you may feel you need additional support with at this time, any opportunities to develop your skills and knowledge, and any threats that might impact negatively on your role and performance.

A photocopiable sheet for completing a SWOT analysis is provided on the previous page. Once you have completed the SWOT analysis, you will probably better understand what support you need going forward. After reading the relevant chapters of this handbook, if you continue to have concerns regarding specific areas, such as your understanding of self-harm, depression or anxiety, and need to develop your skills and knowledge base, it will be helpful to discuss this with your line manager to seek further training.

If part of your role is delivering any small-group interventions or undertaking any one-to-one work with children and young people, it is important to *always access support from someone who can help you to process your own responses, reflect on your practice and ensure that you are responding in the most ethical and appropriate way*. This also involves being very clear about setting up regular supervision sessions or peer-group support sessions where you can discuss any of your concerns and identify needs for future professional development. Being clear about safeguarding protocols within your school context is also essential.

REFLECTION POINT

Take some time now to consider the following questions, which aim to prompt your thinking about your role and also to provide you with an opportunity to clarify your own professional development needs at this time.

- How are children and students in your school setting identified as needing support?

- How do you provide support to pupils in a preventative way to promote wellbeing?

- How do you support student mental health through your everyday interactions?

- What kind of wellbeing and mental health interventions are available in your school that children could be signposted to?

- If you are delivering interventions yourself, do you feel skilled in delivering these interventions and, if not, what kind of support do you need right now?

- What kind of skills do you need to take on the role of the therapeutic, listening adult?

- Are the lines of communication clear within your school in terms of supporting mental health?

- How do you ensure ethical and safe practice? What guidance have you been given to ensure you remain safe in your work? What is your understanding of the importance of not engaging in self-disclosure, being clear about your own boundaries, and managing difficult conversations in which children or young people divulge that they are putting themselves at risk?

- How do you access supervision and support?

- How do you use tools of self-reflection, and why is being a reflective practitioner essential for supporting the wellbeing of children and young people?

- How do you keep yourself well and engage in appropriate levels of self-care? You may need to refer to Chapter 14 at this point, to consider what you might include in your daily wellbeing routines.

CASE STUDY

'When I first started working as a teaching assistant, I was asked to support a boy who was really demotivated. His teacher told me that he was lazy and that I needed to keep on top of him. He often had his head on the desk and got told off a lot. He seemed like he hated school and barely got any work done. On one occasion, he was sent out of the room for ignoring the teacher when she asked him to get his head off the desk. When I followed him out, he burst out crying, and I was actually really shocked because it made me realize that I had never seen any emotion from him at all. I don't think I'd ever seen him smile in the whole six months I'd been working with him. I'd just been too busy nagging him to think about what was going on for him and why he was so demotivated.

'We went for a walk to help him to calm down and he opened up about how low he was feeling. I felt really angry at myself for not having realized and frustrated that I was doing this job without having had any training in mental health and what to look out for. I know now that there were so many warning signs for depression that I wish that I had known to look out for. I also panicked during that discussion because I wanted to find out if he was self-harming and if he was feeling suicidal, but I had no idea if that was okay to ask. What if I asked him and it put the idea into his head? I was worried that I'd get into trouble, so I didn't, I just let him talk, which I guess was helpful.

'I went to speak to the designated senior mental health lead afterwards, and luckily the boy got the support he needed. I told her that I wanted to do more training to understand signs of mental health problems and what to do, so I could do the best for the students, but also so I never have to feel that way again. Not knowing what to do or say felt really scary. We now have posters around the school as reminders of how to respond, and we all have a buddy we can talk to about things like this, so I never feel like I'm in it on my own. It also means I can offload and don't have to take all of my worries about the students home with me.' (Teigan, teaching assistant)

Questions

1. In what ways can you empathize with Teigan's concerns?

2. What questions does this case study raise for you?

The importance of reflective practice

REFLECTION POINT

What is reflective practice and why is it so important? It's a good idea to spend some time considering this as it is particularly crucial when supporting pupils with their emotional needs.

Reflection is a systematic reviewing process critical for all working in the school system. It allows you to make links and learn from one experience to the next, ensuring your practice is constantly developing and improving. For example, you might consider what may not have gone so well during an interaction with a young person in distress and what would help you support other pupils more effectively in the future.

A *reflective practitioner* looks for ways to improve practice by asking for feedback from pupils and colleagues and using new research or theories to inform and improve practice. This might involve reading this handbook or engaging in training, and then using this to improve how you support children and young people.

Reflective practice:

- helps you to feel confident in supporting mental health

- ensures that you are safe and responsible in your interactions with your pupils

- encourages you to learn new skills

- results in better outcomes for pupils.

Key benefits of reflective practice for you
Self-awareness
Through engaging in reflective practice, we can gain a better understanding of our own values and attitudes; we can stand back to evaluate a situation more objectively, putting our own views and biases to one side. This allows us to better support our pupils and colleagues, with greater clarity of thought.

Evaluation leads to evolution

By evaluating and developing our practice, we avoid getting stuck in a rut of always saying and doing the same thing with the same outcome. To continue our professional development, in an ever-changing situation, it is necessary to critically review our practices and knowledge, to recognize areas for growth. This ability to step back and evaluate practice helps us to remain critical and open, not just relying on the tried and tested ways of doing things.

Creating a space for deep thinking

This helps us to hold back from making assumptions or jumping to conclusions. While the pace of change in schools can sometimes feel unrelenting – with many of us often being asked to do more, faster and with fewer resources – it is important to find time to think (even if that sounds like a luxury).

Some common initial concerns about reflective practice are shown in Table 2.1.

Table 2.1 Common initial concerns about reflective practice

Statement	MYTH/ REALITY	Explanation
'It doesn't directly impact my practice if I think about things after I have done them.'	MYTH	Your reflections will directly affect the next interaction or intervention as you learn and develop your skills.
'Reflection takes too long – I do not have the time.'	MYTH	See 'Top tips and strategies' section to avoid believing this assumption.
'Reflection is only focused on me; it does not directly affect the children.'	MYTH	The actions taken in response to your reflections will directly affect your pupils as you change and adapt your approach.
'Reflection is a negative process.'	MYTH	It is a cyclical process, meaning you grow and adapt, resulting in positive change. It offers the opportunity to reflect on what went well and what could be better.

'Reflection is a solo process, so how will I know I've improved?'	MYTH	Reflection should trigger discussion and cooperation; it can feed into the supervision process and inform your supervision sessions. See Chapter 15 'Supervision and Peer Support'.

Top tips and strategies
Standing in someone else's shoes

Gibbs' reflective cycle (1988), inspired partly by Kolb's (1984) learning cycle, enables us to focus on our own and others' feelings, views and perceptions. It provides an opportunity to think more deeply about an interaction and consider how it could be developed in the future. The process is essentially a cycle or loop, as shown in Figure 2.1.

FIGURE 2.1 GIBBS' REFLECTIVE CYCLE (ADAPTED FROM GIBBS, 1988)

This cycle encourages us to reflect on our experiences objectively or from standing in another person's shoes. By doing this, we can look at the situation with new eyes and less emotion, allowing us to learn from it and act. The reflective process requires us to look beneath the surface of our experiences, to achieve more profound levels of reflection and learning.

You may wish to use this process regularly or target one or two situations every couple of weeks that you want to reflect on in more depth. It is important that this becomes a natural process and does not take up copious amounts of your time: if it becomes something laboursome, you will not engage in it and the additional stress would defeat the purpose.

To make this easier, you may well decide to record your thoughts as you work through the process, or jot down notes on a pre-prepared reflection format. In essence, like most learning experiences, this needs to be bespoke to your needs at any given time.

Many in education and the caring professions will engage in journalling to develop their reflective practice. We strongly advise this model as, once again, it can be tailored to suit your own needs, and you can write down or record as much or as little as you think necessary on any given occasion.

Keeping a learning journal

The idea behind keeping a journal is to raise awareness of things that need to be changed so that you can move forward. A learning journal can help you take stock and evaluate a learning experience at your own pace.

A learning journal allows the individual to make notes about an experience. This supports the process of making sense of what we do and how we think and feel about it all. It can also provide you with a resource to further reflect with your line manager. There are different styles of learning journals, including:

- note-taking and sense-making

- guided questions

- picture journal.

Note-taking and sense-making

Think about what happened and what it means, and make notes of your thoughts. When thinking about what happened, you might ask yourself:

- What actually happened?

- Where?

- When?

- Who?

Then in considering what it means, you might reflect on the following:

- What went well?

- What didn't go so well?

- How did you feel?

- How do you imagine that the child felt?

- What could have been done differently?

Guided questions

Some people prefer to have questions to start with rather than a blank page, which could feel intimidating. Questions to ask include:

- What happened?

- How do I feel about it (before, during, after)?

- What insights have I gained through this experience (e.g. about self and others)?

- What will I do the same/differently because of this experience?

Picture journal

Drawing a picture may be useful for demonstrating an experience/ event and supporting you in reflecting. The picture may represent the experience or your feelings about it. Once again, this is entirely down to you. Ultimately, what matters is that you choose the process that best meets your needs and, therefore, works for you.

References

Amir, N., Stafford, J., Freshman, M.S. & Foa, E.B. (1998) 'Relationship between trauma narratives and trauma pathology.' *Journal of Traumatic Stress, 11*, 385–392.

Freud, S. (1920) *A General Introduction to Psychoanalysis*. New York, NY: Boni and Liveright.

Geddes, H. (2006) *Attachment in the Classroom*. London: Worth.

Gibbs, G. (1988) *Learning by Doing: A Guide to Teaching and Learning Methods*. Oxford: Further Education Unit, Oxford Polytechnic.

Kolb, D.A. (1984) *Experiential Learning: Experience as the Source of Learning and Development, Vol. 1.* Englewood Cliffs, NJ: Prentice-Hall.

Sunderland, M. (2022) *Helping Children and Teenagers Talk About Their Lives Using the Arts and the Danger of Un-storied Emotions* [Video] www.childmentalhealthcentre. org/webinars/webinars-single-viewers/product/111-helping-children-and-young-people-talk-about-their-lives-using-arts-and-the-danger-of-un-storied-emotions

CHAPTER 3

Developing Listening Skills

'The most important thing in communication is hearing what isn't said.' (Peter Drucker)

'When people talk, listen completely. Most people never listen.' (Ernest Hemingway)

'Most people do not listen with the intent to understand; they listen with the intent to reply.' (Stephen R. Covey)

Good listening skills are essential when working with children and young people who display social, emotional and mental health difficulties. Many of them will not have felt heard previously, and, in our view, healing and change can only occur within the safety of truly nurturing relationships.

What is effective listening?

Effective listening is an activity that helps the speaker feel understood. It involves the listener actually *hearing* rather than *assuming* what is said. Active listening differs from passive listening, which is attentive but does nothing to assist the speaker. Active listeners maintain attention and eye contact, concentrate fully on what the other person is saying, make small verbal responses to encourage the flow, and summarize parts of what has been said to check understanding and draw together the key parts and allow these to be heard back by the speaker.

Good listeners must give their full attention to hear and really understand what is being said without becoming distracted by the speaker's mannerisms, gestures, accent, dress or delivery. They must avoid becoming overwhelmed by the emotions that are being shared and not allow themselves to drift into thinking about how they will respond. Listeners also need to avoid allowing first impressions of a speaker to cloud their ability to hear the message without judgement. Again, this is where your skills of reflection will be critical in terms of analysing your own skill set in this area and also how you may or may not prejudge individuals when you begin to interact with them.

We cannot learn anything from others if we try to do all the talking. Aim for them to be the ones talking for at least 75 percent of the time. Let speakers finish their own sentences. Don't interrupt them to interject your own thoughts. Ask open questions. Reflect back their thoughts to them. Pay attention to the tone of the words and the nonverbal cues of the speaker. Sometimes, these speak louder than the words themselves. For example, a young person might be telling you that they are not upset, but their tone or body language might be telling you otherwise.

Developing your good listening

An emotionally literate person is someone who is a good listener. As skilled communicators, many school staff consider themselves to be good listeners. However, if we take the time to reflect on our communication with children and young people, we may find that our skills are not as highly developed as we like to think.

Affirming others

Listening is an extremely powerful way of affirming another person. We know that, as children grow, the quality of listening that the adults give them is vital for their psychological development and mental health (Robson, Brogaard-Clausen & Hargreaves, 2017). *Those that have been well listened to are not only likely to feel accepted by others, but they are also more likely to be able to accept themselves*. They have also been given the opportunity to safely express and explore the way that they feel about things and people and this, in turn, helps them to acquire that capacity of inner listening – that is, listening to themselves and being able to trust their own feelings and their own reactions.

That is an essential part of what we would define as *outer listening* (i.e. the ability to listen to others). It is the children who have not been adequately listened to who are likely to be out of touch with their feelings; they are also more likely to be afraid and anxious, and even aggressive and violent at times. So, good listening can affirm the core of another person's being, but poor listening can totally disconfirm it. We have a real duty, as teachers and professionals working with children in the educational field, to ensure that we do not perpetuate this kind of psychological violence. It is therefore vital that we continue to develop and reflect on our skill set in this very important area.

REFLECTION POINT

- Who do you go to when you feel upset or worried about something?

- Why do you tend to choose that person?

- What do you want from them when you are telling them your problem?

Active listening

Active listening, showing empathy and offering validation can help to calm the child or young person, allowing them to feel understood and helping them to express and understand their emotions. This fits within the 'E' (Empathize and listen) section of the FIRES Framework described in Chapter 1. It is essential to allow time and space for this, and always ensure that you have done this step before moving on to 'S' (Support and signpost).

When talking to a child or young person, the following may be helpful:

- Seek information about the situation so you know how to help. Reassure them that that they do not need to retell their story in detail unless they say they want to. Pay attention to tone of voice, body language and establishing good eye contact.

- Listen carefully to what people say and clarify your understanding by repeating back or summarizing what you hear they are trying to communicate.

- Demonstrate you are listening by using nods, murmurs or

encouragers such as 'Oh?' or 'Okay' or 'I understand' – respond without judging.

- Be sensitive and focused; good communication with a distressed child does not require probing into their experience. Accept and support emotions.

- Use language that is simple, direct and easy to understand; speak slowly and calmly; try not to use euphemisms; offer hope; have patience, leaving gaps for them to start speaking.

- Exercise patience if people are confused or find it difficult to explain. Tell them it is okay if they do not want to talk or tell their story; be respectful and compassionate.

Table 3.1 identifies some helpful phrases that you could use in your conversations.

Table 3.1 Helpful phrases

Purpose	Helpful phrases	
Reflect concerns and experiences	'I understand your feelings and lots of people are feeling similarly to you about what's happened/the situation...' 'It is very natural to be sad, angry, upset or...' 'I hear what you are saying, about having to...'	
Explore concerns	'Tell me a bit about what worries you.' 'Is there anything else that worries you?' 'I sense that there is something more on your mind...'	
Normalize and name reactions	'In this situation, how you are feeling and how you want to react is very natural...' [to parent] 'Many parents would be finding this situation difficult, but you have managed to look after your family so far and are able to ask for help when you need it.'	
Clarify what they are saying	'It sounds like you are saying/ feeling...' 'What I'm hearing is... Is that right?' 'That sounds like you're feeling...?'	
Provide affirmations	'Coming to talk to me must have taken a lot of courage.' 'Dealing with that must have been so hard. It sounds to me like you've been very brave and shown a lot of strength.'	

So, we know that good listening is purposeful and focused, requiring motivation and effort. Listening, and really hearing, means paying attention, not only to the story, but how it is told, and what is communicated in the person's body language and tone of voice. In other words, it means being aware of both verbal and nonverbal messages.

Verbal and nonverbal signs of active listening

It is very uncomfortable to be talking to someone and then realize that they are not really listening. They may glance at the clock behind you or start looking at their phone. They may also give verbal signals, or a lack of verbal signals, that let you know that are not really hearing and paying attention to what you are saying. If you have ever had this happen to you, you will know how difficult it is to continue to talk, knowing that the other person is not actively engaged with you. This is the last thing that we want to do to children in distress, who may have taken a long time to build up the courage to talk to you about their feelings. *Turning your body towards them, nodding, asking open questions and maintaining eye contact can all signal to a child that you are actively listening to them.*

REFLECTION POINT

Think about a time when you did not feel listened to and try to identify how this made you feel. What was it, specifically, about the other person's behaviour that made you feel uncomfortable? What did they do that you would regard as 'bad' listening? Also, think about your own interactions and times when you may not have listened well, showed a lack of interest through your body language or simply tried to pre-empt what the other person was going to say. As ever, the way in which we improve our skills is to reflect on them and then plan to change our behaviour when we need to.

CASE STUDY

'An educational psychologist came and did some training with us on active listening, and it was really enlightening. We took turns at talking about an issue whilst the other person practised their active listening skills. Even though it was only for ten minutes, it was so lovely to have the space to talk and be really listened to. It made me realize that, in most conversations, people are just waiting to jump in with their own stories or relating it to their own lives! It was incredible how some of the techniques, such as just repeating back a few of my words, allowed me to reflect on how I really felt. Hearing my own words back made me really think about how I was actually feeling. It allowed me to get the issue straight in my head myself. I didn't need anyone else to solve the problem for me – I just needed to be listened to. It was so powerful. When I then came to practise the techniques on my partner, it was a bit of an adjustment, but it was liberating to free myself from thinking about what advice I should give! One thing that really stuck with me was that the person with the problem should be doing at least 75 percent of the talking. They also said that whenever you think about giving advice, stop yourself and ask an open question instead. That has really helped.' (Tom, head of year)

Questions

1. What techniques did Tom learn about?

2. Which of these do you need to incorporate more into your practice?

Top tips and strategies

There are many strategies you can adopt to help develop your effective listening skills.

Face the speaker and maintain eye contact

In the majority of Western cultures, eye contact is considered to be an indicator of good listening. In general, when we talk, we look each other in the eye. However, be mindful that some children may find eye contact uncomfortable and may prefer that you show that you are listening through sharing attention with the young person in another direction. For example, talking whilst playing a game, or both sitting together and drawing. Equally, some children and young people may prefer that you sit alongside them to talk, rather than opposite them. This might mean that you make eye contact in a more fleeting way, but you can show your attention in other ways. This is particularly true for children and young people on the autism spectrum, those who have experienced trauma or have significant attachment difficulties. It is therefore really important to know the young person's background and history so that you can make sure you remain focused while allowing them to respond in whatever way they feel comfortable. This may well be by not giving you eye contact, simply because this is too threatening for them at the very start of your relationship with them.

Keep an open mind

Always listen with an open mind and try not to question or judge the things that they are saying to you. You may think that their perception of a situation is incorrect, or that their concerns are trivial or irrational. However, those worries feel very real to them, and it important to respect their feelings and try to put yourself in their position. If what they say alarms or worries you, it is important that you remain calm and non-judgemental, and that you do not show any distress. If you do, it is likely to make the young person feel that they are not safe and that you cannot cope with their frightening feelings.

Don't be a 'sentence-grabber'

Occasionally, it can be tempting to try and speed up someone else's thinking by trying to finish their sentences and interrupting them before they have had a chance to make their point. It is really important not to be a 'sentence-grabber' and to wait patiently. Give the child or young person time to process what they want to say so that you don't risk putting words into their mouth or making assumptions.

Listen to the words and try to picture what the speaker is saying

Allow your mind to create a mental representation of the narrative that they are giving you. When listening for longer periods of time, it is important to maintain your concentration and try to remember any key words or phrases the speaker has made use of. It is okay to take some notes if you need to, as long as this does not create a barrier to the young person being able to express themselves. It may also be very useful for making a written record for safeguarding purposes if needed.

Whilst listening, try to avoid spending the time planning what to say next. Think only about what the other person is saying.

Don't interrupt and don't impose your 'solutions'

Although it is useful to interact by clarifying, making encouraging noises and asking open questions, it is also important not to jump in and interrupt. This is particularly so when working with children and young people who are vulnerable and may have been building up to expressing their needs or wants to you. Confiding in someone can take a lot of courage, so it's vital that you allow them to speak without jumping in.

Interrupting sends a variety of messages. It says:

- 'I am more important than you.'

- 'I know better than you.'

- 'What I have to say is more interesting, accurate or relevant.'

- 'I don't care about what you think.'

- 'I don't have time for this conversation.'

- 'This isn't a conversation, it's a contest, and I'm going to be the winner.'

It is important to remember that we all think and speak at different rates. If you are a quick thinker and articulate in expressing yourself, relax your pace for a vulnerable, emotional child or young person who may have difficulty in expressing themselves.

When listening to someone talk about a problem, it is very important to refrain from suggesting solutions straight away. The child or young person will ask for advice if they think they need it, just as an adult would. Sometimes, merely the act of speaking aloud, being heard by someone, can help us to process the problem and find a solution for ourselves. What the speaker really needs is for you to simply listen and support them to make their own plan. This is crucial in helping the young person to feel heard and understood. Only then can you start to think about support, signposting and solutions. Following the FIRES Framework will help you to avoid this common mistake.

Ask the right questions

Asking questions can help to clarify and ensure an accurate understanding. For example, a clarifying question might range from a full sentence such as 'It sounds as though you felt really angry with your mum...', to just a short phrase or repeating something that they have said back to them, inviting them to reflect and clarify, 'You hate your mum?'

You may also ask open questions to allow the child or young person to fully express themselves and explore the situation from different viewpoints. For example:

- How did that make you feel?

- How do you think your mum was feeling?

- Why do you think that she was angry? Is there anything else that she might have been feeling?

Try to feel what the speaker is feeling

To experience empathy, you have to put yourself in the other person's place and allow yourself to feel what it is like to *be them* at that particular moment. This is not always easy, but it will help the person to feel that you are connecting with them, which will help them to cope with the emotions that are overwhelming them. The child or young person needs to know that you are there with them in that feeling, and that the feelings that they have are valid and accepted.

Reflect back their feelings

Show that you understand the child or young person and help them to understand their feelings by labelling them and reflecting them back; for example, 'It sounds as though that experience was really frightening for you...' or 'I can see that you are overwhelmed...'. Labelling these emotions aloud will help the young person to understand how they are feeling and reduce the intensity of those feelings. We will talk more about this in Chapter 5 'Emotion Coaching'.

Pay attention to what isn't said (nonverbal cues)

You can tell as much, if not more, about how someone is feeling by their body language, tone and gestures, in comparison with the words that they are saying. In fact, our body language often gives away truths that we sometimes don't want to express verbally because we are less conscious of them and do not choose them as carefully as we might choose our words. When you are listening to a young person, it is also crucial to look out for other clues as to how they feel through what they are showing you.

Activity – The Bad/Good Listener Checklists

Have a go at this activity, and then discuss with a friend, colleague or your line manager, identifying what you may need to develop in your own listening.

The Bad Listener Checklist
When listening, do you sometimes:

- interrupt

- get distracted

- listen with half your attention

- glance at your phone or watch if you receive an alert

- think about what you want to say and wait for the chance to say it

- stare into space

- give advice and offer solutions that have not been asked for

- ignore body language cues

- jump in with your own experiences and views?

The Good Listener Checklist
When listening, do you:

- ensure that the speaker has your full attention

- empathize and validate the child or young person

- summarize what you've heard

- ask open questions

- allow them to do most of the speaking?

REFLECTION POINT

1. Think of at least three individuals in your current or past life that you would regard as being really good at listening, and three that you consider to be very poor at listening.

2. On one half of a sheet of A4 paper, write down all the characteristics you associated with good listeners and, on the other side of the page, all of those that you associated with bad listeners.

3. Have a short period of self-reflection, assessing your own skills, resources and deficits as a listener. Looking at these two lists, which ones would apply to you and which ones do you think you could change? What do you need to do in order to make such changes?

Reference

Robson, S., Brogaard-Clausen, S. & Hargreaves, D. (2017) 'Loved or listened to? Parent and practitioner perspectives on young children's well-being.' *Early Child Development and Care, 189*(7), 1147–1161.

CHAPTER 4

Understanding Attachment and Developmental Trauma

What is attachment?

Attachment is the emotional bond that forms between an infant and their caregiver. John Bowlby, a famous psychologist, developed his attachment theory (1958) based on observations he made when children were separated from their parents during World War 2. Even when the children were placed with loving families, he noticed the detrimental impact this separation had on the social and emotional wellbeing of the children. He suggested that throughout the first few years of their lives, a baby's primary way of getting their needs met is through crying or distress. In most cases, these needs are predictably and consistently met by their caregiver, and the baby learns who is the most responsive and attuned to their needs. This first attachment is usually made at around seven months, when the baby starts to show a clear preference for a caregiver and becomes distressed when separated from them. Through this process, the baby forms an 'inner working model' or template by which they create their understanding of themselves and those around them. When their needs are met consistently through 'good enough' parenting (Winnicott, 1973), they develop a 'secure' attachment, and they come to understand that:

- they are special and important and can impact the world

- adults are caring, consistent, safe and trustworthy

- the world is a safe place to explore from the safety of their caregivers.

However, when those needs are not met predictably and consistently by an adult attuned to their needs, they are more likely to form an 'insecure' attachment. This means that the baby is likely to be left with very high levels of stress that, without adequate co-regulation from a caregiver, can have a long-lasting impact on their ability to self-regulate. In this situation, the template that the child develops is one in which they feel that:

- they are not special and important

- adults are unsafe, untrustworthy and unpredictable

- the world is dangerous and full of threats that they are not protected from.

Following their first attachment, babies make multiple other attachments, usually within the first year of life. The first three years are considered a particularly 'sensitive period' during which the infants require predictable, consistent and sensitive care to develop into secure children with good self-esteem and a sense of safety within the world.

It has been estimated that roughly 60 percent of children have a secure attachment, whilst 40 percent are insecurely attached (Moullin, Waldfogel & Washbrook, 2014). This can occur for a range of reasons, including:

- no one interacting (looking/talking/smiling) with the infant for long periods

- not comforting the child when they are crying and leaving them to 'cry it out'

- the child's needs being met some days and not others (the child does not know what behaviour to expect)

- separation from family, particularly during the first three years

- repeated changes of primary caregiver

- persistent disregard for the child's basic physical needs

- continual exposure to a range of external stressors (family conflict, abuse, domestic violence, parental drug use, mental illness).

According to Moullin et al. (2014), 40 percent of insecurely attached children fall into the following categories, which were originally identified by Ainsworth and Bell (1970):

- *Anxious-avoidant* (25%) – The infant shuts down and detaches from people. The child develops feelings of not being good enough, withdraws from close relationships, suppresses painful negative memories, and fails to acknowledge negative feelings. They are likely to develop a belief in the need for self-reliance.

- *Anxious-ambivalent* (15%) – The infant exacerbates their distress due to the belief that they have to magnify their emotions to receive support. They are intermittently rewarded for such behaviour with attention from an attachment figure. The child craves attachment and is likely to experience fear and anger towards others for not providing care.

The attachment classification tends to remain the same (be it secure, avoidant or ambivalent). However, if the relationship between the child and their primary/secondary attachment figure changes, the classification can change as well.

REFLECTION POINT
Think about your own bonds in early childhood and consider the extent to which you felt safe and nurtured or otherwise. It is important to recognize your attachment style and how this may or may not have impacted your development and relationships, both in the past and now. What impact do you think your experiences may have had on the ways you interact now with children and young people?

What is trauma?

Trauma is the emotional response to a distressing experience that is sudden and unpredictable and feels beyond our control. Traumatic events are those that shake our sense of safety in the world. Common traumatic events include the loss of a parent in childhood, sexual abuse, violence or the unexpected loss of a loved one. Of course, we can now also highlight the *trauma resulting from the COVID-19 pandemic – on children, young people and adults*. The psychological effects of trauma may include emotional distress, painful memories and anxiety. The shock and loss of feelings of security can lead to numbness and difficulty connecting with others.

Experiencing trauma frequently stems from situations posing a threat to life or safety; however, any circumstance causing a sense of overwhelming isolation can lead to trauma. It is crucial to recognize that the traumatic nature of an event is not solely determined by the external circumstances but is instead influenced by our emotional response to it. The greater our feelings of fear, isolation and helplessness during an event, the higher the likelihood of experiencing trauma as an aftermath.

Trauma can be caused by:

- *single events* – accidents, injuries, surgery (especially early in life), sudden death of a loved one, witnessing something shocking, the break-up of a relationship or experiencing violence

- *chronic stress* – growing up in an environment that feels unsafe, having a life-threatening illness or experiencing repeated traumatic events, such as bullying, abuse, domestic violence, being repeatedly shamed or humiliated by someone or neglect (we would place the recent COVID-19 pandemic under this heading given the ongoing nature of the disruption).

The effects of early childhood trauma on emotional development

Traumatic events can have an overwhelming and long-lasting sensory impact on children. Due to such frightening experiences, visual stimuli, loud noises and sudden movements can make them feel unsafe. You may find that children are hypervigilant to possible threats around them and may suffer with phobias and nightmares. Young children may be affected in a particularly profound way as they are unable to accurately comprehend the relationship between cause and effect. They may think that they are to blame in some way, or that their wishes or thoughts have come true and caused the traumatic event.

Young children are also less able to predict when something may happen, are less likely to be prepared and have less control over the event, making them more vulnerable to trauma. To compound this, young children's brains are developing rapidly and are therefore particularly vulnerable. Through the relationships that children have with their caregivers and their experiences, they are forming an understanding of the world and creating neural pathways between the emotional part of the brain and the cerebral cortex. This part of the brain is responsible for reasoning, rational thought, logic, planning, attention and language. Research suggests that trauma in early childhood is associated with reduced size of the cerebral cortex, resulting in impairment to executive functioning skills such as planning, attention and working memory, as well as emotional regulation (Jeong et al., 2021).

Another reason that young children are so vulnerable to trauma is that they are reliant upon their parents or caregivers for their safety. If the trauma also impacts the parent – for example, a bereavement within the family – the ability of the parent or caregiver to be emotionally available for the child can be compromised. This can result in the child being overwhelmed by a level of stress that they are unable to regulate or communicate effectively. This can lead to changes in behaviour (e.g. clinginess, difficulty sleeping, relationship-seeking), increased emotional distress (e.g. anxiety, fear, aggression, impulsivity) and regressions (e.g. wetting the bed, frequent night-waking).

Distressing events activate the brain's fear centre, the amygdala (with its name originating from the Greek for 'almond' due to its shape). The amygdala sends an alert to other areas of the brain to signal a threat and prepare the body for a fight-or-flight response. The sympathetic nervous system leaps into action, releasing adrenaline and noradrenaline and triggering the physiological symptoms associated with fear and anxiety (racing heart, faster breathing, trembling limbs, nausea, etc.). Usually, these feelings subside after the event, and the memories of the experience fade over time. However, as said previously, it is not the event that causes the trauma; it is how the person experienced it. If the experience was particularly shocking, sudden, out of the person's control and they felt alone, it is more likely that the negative feelings may continue and impact on the child's life for a longer period of time.

How does this show up in behaviour in school?

For the child in school who has suffered trauma, there are clear implications for attention, behaviour and access to learning. In the classroom, this can have many presentations, including:

- not feeling safe in the classroom

- prone to 'fight-or-flight' reactions

- difficulty regulating their emotions
- hypervigilant to threats
- mistrust of adults
- relationship-seeking behaviours
- testing boundaries
- difficulties with relationships and friendships
- low self-esteem
- difficulty accepting praise
- limited academic progress
- attention and concentration difficulties.

Resilience and protective factors

Whilst young children are more vulnerable to experiencing trauma following a distressing event, it is not always the case. Research in the field of resilience has found that there are certain protective factors that enhance the child's ability to respond with resilience in the aftermath of a potentially traumatic incident. In particular, the presence of a warm, consistent, emotionally available adult, who can be there for the child or young person, provide reassurance and encourage them to talk, can shield children against trauma following adversity (Peterson, Tuppett & Yates, 2013). Often, this is a parent, carer or family member. *However, in many cases, this may be a teacher, teaching assistant or other adult within the school that can provide this invaluable support for a child or young person.*

An optimistic approach

We know from research on neuroplasticity that with the proper support, new neural pathways can be formed, and the impact of trauma can be reduced. Even when the trauma happened many years prior, steps can be taken to form a relationship with the young person, develop trust and feelings of safety, and help them start to regulate their emotions (Thomaes et al., 2014).

CASE STUDY

'Hamid started at our school when he was six years old, having moved across the country with his mum and sister to get away from his violent stepfather. His behaviour seemed to be very confident in some ways, because he liked to be in control, and he was quite loud. However, he was in a constant state of fight-or-flight, and it was a struggle just to keep him in the classroom. He kept running away and climbing up a tree. It was like he wanted to do things that were dangerous because he knew they would get a response from the adults.

'Loud noises, changes in routine and making mistakes in his work were huge triggers for Hamid. Often, he wouldn't even attempt the work because he was terrified that he wouldn't be able to do it, and that wasn't a feeling that he could cope with at that time. He showed lots of relationship-seeking behaviours and wanted my attention at all times. We knew that he had been through a huge amount of trauma in his short life, including witnessing domestic abuse, being subject to emotional abuse, abandonment by his biological father, his stepfather having an addiction, and his mother having a mental health issue. To add to that, he was now suffering the loss of his relationship with his stepfather, a house move and change of school.

'We decided to take the approach of having a key adult for Hamid, who would be available at all times during the school day to form a relationship with him, attune to his emotions, help him to self-regulate and feel safe within the school environment. I was fortunate enough to be chosen to be Hamid's key adult, given that we had already established a bond. It has been challenging at times, and Hamid has often tried to test the boundaries and push me away, but I know it is just because he hasn't learned that adults can be safe, consistent and predictable.

'Quite quickly, Hamid seemed more comfortable in the classroom environment and stopped running away. He still needs space sometimes, but this is one of his strategies to self-regulate and he goes to an agreed safe place. This mostly happens when the teacher raises his voice. We are a year on now, and Hamid has made friends, is enjoying school and is making progress with his learning. The next step will be to start to develop his independence, but I am confident that he now feels safe enough in school to move on to that next challenge.' (Heloise, teaching assistant)

Questions

1. What signs of trauma can you see in Hamid's behaviour?

2. How do you think these kinds of behaviours are sometimes interpreted in schools?

3. What were Hamid's triggers in school?

4. What support was particularly helpful for Hamid?

Top tips and strategies
Helping children and young people to self-regulate

Children and young people who have experienced trauma all have one thing in common – a loss of their sense of safety. The strategies below can help children and young people to regulate their emotions, build connections, feel safe and heal from the trauma.

The '3 Rs' approach (Perry and Dobson, 2013) provides a framework and rationale for the importance of helping children to regulate first, before trying to relate or reason with them. The '3 Rs' are:

*   *Regulate* – When a person becomes very distressed, they may move into survival mode and show behaviours such as 'fight, flight or freeze'. When in this state, our ability to rationalize, use logic, reason and relate to others is impaired. We must first calm the stress response, and this can often be achieved through rhythmic, repetitive and soothing tasks. Consider our instinct when soothing a baby or young child. We do not try to reason with them, but instead, we hold their heads close to our heart beat, we rock, sway, pat and 'shh' to soothe them. Whilst we cannot necessarily do all of these for the children and young people that we work with, we can use the same principle to find other rhythmic and soothing activities, such as breathing strategies, walking or listening to calming music.

*   *Relate* – Once regulated, we can reconnect with the child or young person to help them to feel safe, accepted and understood. Listening is the greatest tool at your disposal and, given that the child or young person is likely to still be in a heightened

state, your body language, tone of voice and demeanour are as important as the words you say, if not more so.

- *Reason* – Reasoning is only likely to be possible once the child or young person is in a calm state, in which they feel safe. At this point, the child may be able to reflect upon the situation and problem-solve.

Self-regulation strategies include:

- *Movement* – One of the effects of trauma can be that the young person is likely in a fight-or-flight state for much of the time. Exercise and movement can help to rebalance the nervous system, by using the adrenaline and releasing endorphins to help the person to feel calmer and happier. Rhythmic exercise, such as running, walking, basketball or dancing, is considered particularly beneficial, as the sensory input can help the body self-regulate. Try giving frequent sensory movement breaks throughout the day to help the young person remain in balance. During these breaks, help keep the young person grounded by adding some mindfulness practice. Encourage them to notice what they can hear, how their temperature changes as they move, where their body feels tense, and so on.

- *Breathing* – Even when a child feels completely out of control, it can be of great comfort to know that we can bring our nervous system back into balance simply through our breathing. Not only will this relieve the anxiety that they are likely to be feeling, but it can also help them to feel more in control.

  - Hot chocolate breathing: Take a deep breath in through the nose, pretending to smell the delicious hot chocolate, and then a long, slow, steady out-breath to try to cool the hot chocolate down.

  - Star breathing: Imagine tracing your finger around the outline of a star shape. Every time you go up on one of the points, you breathe in for four seconds, and then as you trace your finger down the point, you breathe out for four seconds.

- *Calming the senses* – It may be that there are some sights, sounds, smells or textures that help the young person to feel calm. These will be different for everyone, but you might find that stroking an animal or teddy, the smell of lavender or their parent's scarf, or some calming classical music helps them to relax.

The importance of relationships

After experiencing trauma, a young person may want to withdraw from others, but isolation is likely to make things worse. They may also find it difficult to trust others and feel safe within relationships. However, relationships and connections with others are key protective factors that help a person respond with resilience in times of adversity. It is vital to help children to build relationships with adults and with their peers.

Remember that those who have experienced trauma may not want to talk about it, and that's okay. Sometimes, school is the one place they have where they can feel 'normal' and think about other things. Just being there and engaging with them will support recovery by helping them to feel connected. On the other hand, it is important that they have someone to whom they can talk about their feelings. This may be a family member, a friend or an external professional, or within school through play therapy, drawing and talking therapy, for example.

The key adult approach

Having a 'key adult' can provide the child or young person with a consistent, predictable adult who can help to calm their nervous system and regulate their emotions. The key adult should be attuned to the child's emotions and responsive to their needs in order to build trust and develop a positive attachment. The idea is that the key adult becomes the child's 'safe base' from which they then feel safe to learn, develop friendships and take risks. The key adult will 'provide a consistent presence for the child in school, be given time to spend with the child and will be able to check in with them at times of the day that require transition between places or adults' (AFC, 2021).

> 'The relationship between the key adult and the child with attachment difficulties will be pivotal in terms of the child's learning' (Bomber, 2008).

The role of the key adult is to

- understand that relationships, safety and trust are crucial

- use positive language, empathy and emotion coaching

- be consistent, attuned, reliable, attentive, responsive and caring at all times

- provide unconditional positive regard and recognize behaviour as being separate from the child or young person themselves

- advocate for the child and help other adults and peers to understand their thoughts, feelings and behaviour

- provide emotional containment

- understand that all behaviour is communication

- be curious, accepting and patient in order to understand the unmet needs being demonstrated through behaviour

- understand that the child is not attention-seeking; they are attention-needing/relationship-seeking

- model appropriate behaviours and positive social interactions

- be resilient and patient

- understand that the child may test the boundaries of your relationship.

There are a number of simple strategies that you can make use of to support the child or young person to regulate, and to feel safe and secure in their learning and in social contexts. Take a look at the following ideas and consider which ones you might make use of now or in the future:

- *Be predictable and consistent* – Children or young people with insecure attachments, or those who have experienced trauma in their early years, are very sensitive to changes in routine, transitions and unstructured times such as break time, lunchtime and before school. Being predictable and consistent will help the child or young person to feel more secure. This is likely to reduce their anxiety, and the controlling behaviours that they may exhibit as a result.

- *Be patient* – The child or young person may have been let down repeatedly in the past and have a long-held distrust of adults.

They may try to push you away, test boundaries and sabotage the relationship. It is important to stand firm, give unconditional positive regard and always separate the child from their behaviour.

- *Give praise* – Use specific praise and be aware that praise may be difficult for the child to accept as it may not fit with their internal working model of themselves. Be mindful of praising the child publicly and start by offering specific praise privately to the young person to test the water.

- *Take the attitude of 'PACE'* – This stands for Playfulness, Acceptance, Curiosity and Empathy (Golding & Hughes, 2012). Use these principles to guide your interactions with children and young people.

- *Use transitional objects* – These can support the child or young person to still feel connected even when you are not together. Even with older children, they may feel comforted by looking after an object for you until you are reunited.

- *Avoid arguments and power struggles* – Taking the PACE approach and using humour can reduces the student's need for control.

- *Foster a sense of control* – Help children to feel a sense of control and calm by providing choices where possible. For example, rather than saying 'Come and sit on the carpet', you might say, 'Would you like to sit at the front of the carpet, or at the back?'.

- *Avoid showing anger* – Keep calm in response to their distressed behaviours (e.g. refusal to engage, leaving the classroom, aggression). Explain why the behaviours are wrong in a firm but measured way.

- *Provide opportunities to reconnect after conflict* – Conflict can be very distressing for children with attachment needs or who have experienced trauma. Although they may have seemed to push you away, it is important to provide opportunities to reconnect following a conflict once they are calm. This unconditional positive regard reinforces that the pupil can trust you and helps to reduce their feelings of shame.

'I love being a key adult, but it also feels like a huge responsibility. When I'm unwell and need to be away from school, I really panic about how Matthew will cope. I know it's silly and I have to look after myself and my family too, but it makes me feel like I've let him down.' (Trish, teaching assistant)

Creating a calm corner

Establishing a calm tranquil corner, room or space where children and young individuals can acquire skills to regulate themselves safely is now a consideration that all schools can and should undertake. While certain aspects may seem tailored for primary settings, having a secure self-regulation area in a secondary school is equally essential.

The 'Calm Corner' or 'Safe Space' should serve as a special sanctuary where children and young people can cultivate tools and strategies, fostering resilience and self-regulation skills. The primary aim of such a space is to enhance self-awareness, leading to increased adaptability, flexibility and independence. It is important for this area to be a calm, safe space, and vital that it is not also used as a place for punishments or sanctions.

Furthermore, the calm corner can offer solace to those grappling with loss, providing a haven for processing grief or taking a moment for reflection, remembrance and expressing their emotions. This space can serve as a crucial intervention for children and young individuals who have undergone traumatic experiences.

Five tips for setting up a calm corner

- *Tip 1: Location* – Thoughtful consideration should be given to choosing the location for your calm corner. For instance, opting for a discreet area at the back of the classroom can alleviate potential self-consciousness among pupils using it. While having a dedicated room is the optimal choice, it may not be a viable option for many given that space is often at a premium within schools. When choosing the location, consider the following questions:

  - Does the chosen space provide adequate room for a chair, small sofa, bean bag and potentially a small table?

- – Does the space afford enough privacy?

- – Is the area easily accessible for children?

- *Tip 2: Furniture* – The selection of furniture plays a crucial role in establishing your relaxation area. The size of the space will dictate the items you can incorporate. At the very least, ensure there is sufficient seating, such as a chair, bean bag or a small sofa. Additionally, a compact desk or table proves valuable for self-reflection or drawing/colouring/writing activities, while the inclusion of a listening booth facilitates access to music tapes, relaxation tapes or online calming resources.

- *Tip 3: Useful visuals* – You will need to provide pupils with visual aids and resources to help them to self-regulate and manage their emotions. Consider including:

  - – a poster illustrating various breathing techniques

  - – a poster prompting students to assess their 'emotional temperature'

  - – a list suggesting activities they can engage in within the calm corner

  - – a resource outlining step-by-step strategies for problem-solving

  - – a display of mindfulness techniques, such as square breathing or the 5,4,3,2,1 grounding technique.

- *Tip 4: Self-regulation tools* – An integral part of a calm corner is the sensory tools that children can use to help themselves to self-regulate and return to their 'window of tolerance'. For example:

  - – glitter jars/snow globes

  - – squishy balls

  - – sensory sticks

  - – expandable ball

  - – modelling clay

- sand

- timer.

- *Tip 5: Teach children how to use the calm corner* – It is crucial to educate all pupils about the purpose of the calm corner. Understanding why it is a beneficial and essential intervention for our wellbeing is key. Address questions such as: Why do we need it? What is it for? What resources are available in the corner, and how, when and why should we use them? Allocating time for a discussion as a whole class or form group is imperative to reinforce the purpose and practical aspects of the calm corner.

Calming strategies and resources to use in a calm corner

- *Breathing in the right way* – Our breath plays a crucial role in emotion regulation. We will cover this in more detail in Chapter 8. If you believe that focusing on breathing could benefit the child, consider integrating breathing techniques throughout the day. This could occur at the beginning of each school morning and afternoon, at home before departing for school, or as part of the regular routines in your calm corner or nurturing provision/area.

    - Progressive muscular relaxation (PMR): This entails tensing and releasing various body parts, starting at the toes and working upwards to the face, and back down. Muscles are tensed during the in-breath and then released during the out-breath. For younger children, a whole-body tense-and-release approach works well, such as pretending to transform from a robot to a ragdoll.

    - Finger breathing: Extend the fingers of one hand and, while breathing, use the index finger of the other hand to trace around the thumb and fingers. Inhale from the thumb's base to the tip and exhale from the tip to the base on the opposite side, repeating this pattern. This can then be repeated with the other hand.

- *Visualization tools and ideas* – Offer a variety of visualization scripts and work with pupils to help them to create their own. For instance, envision:

- collecting emotions, compressing them, and placing them into a box

- moving away from distressing feelings by walking, swimming, biking or jogging

- treating your thoughts like a disliked song or TV programme, changing the channel or lowering the volume – acknowledging their presence without actively engaging with them.

- *Using a weighted blanket* – Applying deep pressure to the body through a weighted blanket can increase the release of serotonin, a neurotransmitter associated with feelings of wellbeing, in the brain.

- *54321 grounding technique* – Engage the five primary senses to focus attention on the present moment. Encourage children to notice five things they can see, four they can touch, three they can hear, two they can smell and one they can taste. This is easy to teach and a highly effective grounding strategy.

- *Sensory basket* – Making a sensory basket with various scented objects can be an enjoyable and grounding activity (e.g. lavender, lemons, basil, soap, coffee beans, rosemary, etc.).

- *Make sensory 'rain' bottles* – Sensory bottles harness the calming influence of rain sounds to ease a child's concerns and can be made from a wide variety of household items, like dried rice, beads or buttons. Assist the child in adding their selected items to fill approximately half of the container, seal the lid and then enjoy the tranquil sounds.

- Feelings check-in – Have some reflection sheets available for pupils to label and record their feelings, challenge their thoughts and problem-solve. You might also have positive prompts for pupils to identify things that have gone well that day, what they are proud of and who they are grateful to.

All activities and resources will need to be personalized depending upon the pupils' emotional, social and cognitive development, and the sensory profile of individuals that you think will frequently need to use the calm corner. It is important to maintain open communication with the children about what resources and activities they find most helpful in calming down.

References

AFC (2021) Previously Looked-After Children: Key Adults. www.afcvirtualschool previouslylookedafterchildren.org.uk/page/?title=Key+Adults&pid=117

Ainsworth, M. & Bell, S. (1970) 'Attachment, exploration, and separation: Illustrated by the behavior of one-year-olds in a strange situation.' *Child Development, 41*, 49–67.

Bomber, L. (2008) *Inside I'm Hurting.* Brighton: Worth.

Bowlby, J. (1958) 'The nature of the child's tie to his mother.' *International Journal of Psychoanalysis, 39*, 350–373.

Golding, K.S. & Hughes, D.A. (2012) *Creating Loving Attachments: Parenting with PACE to Nurture Confidence and Security in the Troubled Child.* London: Jessica Kingsley Publishers.

Jeong, H.J., Durham, E.L., Moore, T.M., Dupont, R.M. et al. (2021) 'The association between latent trauma and brain structure in children.' *Translational Psychiatry, 11*, 240. doi:10.1038/s41398-021-01357-z

Moullin, S., Waldfogel, J. & Washbrook, L. (2014) *Baby Bonds: Parenting, Attachment and a Secure Base for Children.* London: Sutton Trust.

Perry, B.D. & Dobson, C.L. (2013) 'The Neurosequential Model of Therapeutics.' In J.D. Ford & C.A. Courtois (Eds.), *Treating Complex Traumatic Stress Disorders in Children and Adolescents: Scientific Foundations and Therapeutic Models* (pp.249–260). New York, NY: The Guilford Press.

Peterson, S.M., Tuppett, M. & Yates, T.M. (2013) 'Early Childhood Relationships and the Roots of Resilience.' In R.E Tremblay, M. Boivin & R.DeV. Peters (Eds.), A.S. Masten (Topic Ed.), *Encyclopedia on Early Childhood Development* [online]. www.child-encyclopedia.com/resilience/according-experts/early-childhood-relationships-and-roots-resilience

Thomaes, K., Dorrepaal, E., Draijer, N., Jansma, E.P. et al. (2014) 'Can pharmacological and psychological treatment change brain structure and function in PTSD? A systematic review.' *Journal of Psychiatric Research, 50*, 1–15. doi:10.1016/j.jpsychires.2013.11.002

Winnicott, D.W. (1973) *The Child, the Family, and the Outside World.* London: Penguin.

■ CHAPTER 5 ■

Emotion Coaching

Why is emotion coaching important?

When children show signs of distress and anger, in either the learning or social context, there is often a mirrored response from adults themselves, who might be very wound up and opt to send the child for time-out. This kind of time-out is often not consistent with the trauma-informed approach described in the previous chapter – involving access to a therapeutic adult in a safe space, with opportunities to self-regulate – which, if carried out, would be entirely appropriate. However, in many instances, the old behaviourist approaches, including access to the so-called naughty step, result in children and young people being sent to reflect without additional adult support to help them do so effectively. When children have been treated this way, it is hardly surprising that they enter their teenage years unable to express or talk about their feelings.

However, we now know more about how the brain works and would reject these outdated behaviourist approaches. We understand that it is essential to move away from such approaches to truly ensure that our children can develop the kind of self-regulation they need in both the home and learning contexts.

Sending a child to sit on their own on the naughty step in an attempt to get them to reflect on their behaviours is usually highly counterproductive. Instead of enabling them to talk about how they are feeling, express it and begin to process their feelings, this approach ensures that they do the opposite: bottle up their emotions and not talk about them. This is clearly unhealthy. When we have these overwhelming feelings, we must normalize them in a safe and nurturing context. We do not need to be punished for having these big feelings, but rather to develop the skills to understand and manage them more effectively. *This is why developing emotion coaching skills is essential for school staff working with children and young people of all ages.*

Emotional intelligence – why it matters

We all must learn to understand our emotions and manage them effectively. The term 'emotional intelligence' was introduced by Daniel Goleman in 1995. Since then, researchers have become increasingly aware of how important it is to recognize our emotions and healthily manage them.

Emotional intelligence is learned, and many people prefer the term 'emotional literacy' as a reflection of this. A child's first teachers about emotions are their parents or carers. Still, school staff can also help children develop emotional literacy and regulation by 'coaching' them, using principles researchers have found work well.

Research shows that emotion-coached children (Gottman & DeClaire, 1997):

- are more emotionally stable

- are more resilient

- achieve more academically

- are more popular

- have fewer behavioural problems

- have fewer infectious diseases.

When a child or young person is in a heightened state of anxiety, they very often experience a *panic reaction*. An emotional 'hijack' happens in the brain, meaning that they are not open to reason at that point in time and are very often unable to understand or communicate what they are feeling. When faced with a student in this state who may be running away or being aggressive towards you or others, it is usually very unhelpful to ask *why* they are feeling or behaving in a certain way. This is where emotion coaching becomes the essential go-to technique. As a method of de-escalating such situations and allowing the child or young person to process and understand their emotions, emotion coaching can be an incredibly useful tool to add to your repertoire.

What is emotion coaching?

Gottman & DeClaire (1997) developed the idea of emotion coaching as an approach for parents supporting children with their emotions. They described four different approaches to parenting, as described below.

- *Dismissive* – Parents who use a 'dismissive' style may ignore the emotion, try to distract from it, and do their best to get the negative emotion to go away as soon as possible! This approach is often very well-meaning but low in empathy and guidance. This sends the message to the child that overwhelming emotions are bad and make others uncomfortable.

- *Disapproving* – Adults may punish or criticize the child for their big emotions, by, for example, telling a child to stop crying or 'Pull yourself together'. The approach is very high in guidance but low in empathy. This again tells the child that big emotions are bad and that they should not show their feelings.

- *Laissez-faire* – Translated as 'allow to do'. This parenting style is high in empathy as parents may understand the underlying emotions, but they offer little guidance, coaching, limits or problem-solving opportunities. This does nothing to help the child or young person to understand their feelings and how to regulate them.

- *Emotion coaching* – In contrast, this approach seeks to be high in both empathy and guidance. Parents accept their child's emotions and empathize and validate them. They also guide and coach children by labelling their emotions with them, setting limits where needed and problem-solving. This approach tells children that emotions are okay and that adults are safe. They can cope with their big emotions, and they learn to regulate their emotions through co-regulation with an emotionally available adult.

These styles are summarized in Table 5.1.

Emotion coaching, as an approach, helps children and young people really understand the different emotions that they experience, why they happen, and how they can handle them effectively. In essence, we can coach our children and young people about their emotions by comforting them, listening to them, understanding their thoughts and feelings and supporting them to do likewise. This approach encourages the development of healthy, nurturing and supportive relationships. It also promotes respect and a genuine sense of feeling valued. This emotionally supportive foundation ensures our children and young people can grow into well-balanced adults who can effectively set their own limits and boundaries and problem-solve productively.

Table 5.1 Parenting styles

DISMISSIVE	DISAPPROVING	LAISSEZ-FAIRE	EMOTION COACHING
Wants to relieve the uncomfortable emotion by ignoring, dismissing or distracting Treats feelings as trivial or irrational Relies on passage of time to heal 'You're just tired.' 'Calm down.' 'You're okay.'	Judges, criticizes the child's emotions May punish the child for having big emotions 'Stop crying.' 'That's enough!' 'Boys don't cry.' 'Pull yourself together'	Freely accepts emotions but takes a 'hands-off' approach No limit-setting on behaviour that may result from emotions No problem-solving or repair 'Express your feelings however you need to.' 'I trust you to handle your emotions.' 'You'll figure it out on your own.'	Tolerates and accepts big emotions Sees emotions as an opportunity to connect and teach Listens and empathizes Sets limits and helps to solve problems 'I can tell this is really frustrating you.' 'Would it help if we brainstormed some solutions together?' 'It's okay to feel angry, but it's never okay to hit someone.'

As a member of school staff, working through a challenging situation with a young person will be a regular part of your work. Supporting children and young people in coping with difficult emotions is essential to what you do in your role. It is, therefore, imperative that you not only understand how to use the emotion coaching approach but also clearly understand your own levels of emotional literacy and capacity to manage your feelings effectively.

CASE STUDY

Cameron is 11 years old and dislikes school. He struggles to make friends and feels like everyone is against him all the time. He finds literacy particularly challenging, and he is aware that the gap between him and his peers is growing. Cameron feels like there is something wrong with him and can't understand why everything seems to come so easily to everyone else. Cameron is a young carer for his mother who has Parkinson's disease. He gets the bus home, then needs to clean, help make dinner and look after his younger siblings. This means that it is sometimes difficult for Cameron to do all of his homework on time. However, he doesn't tell anyone about this because he doesn't want to feel more different than he already does.

Cameron is often tired because he shares a room with his younger brother, who frequently wakes him during the night. After a disagreement with his peers one lunchtime, Cameron came to his science lesson feeling particularly unsettled. The teacher gave him a worksheet of equations that looked impossible to him. He swiped it off the desk in frustration and laid his head on the table. The teacher turned around and immediately sent Cameron out of the room. He was sent to the head of year and given an after-school detention as a consequence.

Questions

1. Aside from frustration, what other emotions might have been under the surface for Cameron in that situation?

2. Why was Cameron feeling that way?

3. Will the detention support Cameron with the underlying reasons for his behaviour in the science lesson?

4. What support do you think Cameron needs?

All behaviour is a form of communication; therefore, it is important to recognize and label the feelings underneath the behaviours. Often, children might appear to be angry, but anger can be usefully thought about as a secondary emotion resulting from other feelings beneath the surface. Anger is an active emotion – it allows us to feel more in control and protects us from the feelings below that may make us feel more vulnerable (e.g. shame, guilt, sadness, fear). The anger iceberg is a widely used analogy to illustrate this phenomenon.

FIGURE 5.1 ANGER ICEBERG

REFLECTION POINT

Stop to think about a recent time you felt angry. What was the result? How did you express this? What was really underlying these feelings at the time? Were you stressed, anxious or frightened, perhaps? Could you have expressed yourself differently? What might have helped you? What might you do differently in a similar situation in the future?

How does emotion coaching work?

Emotion coaching is a stepped approach and relatively straightforward. What matters here is that you *understand the need to practise and use it regularly*, if you are going to become skilled as an emotion coach.

It is important to remember that emotion coaching will ultimately reduce stress because it enables you to approach situations and relationships in a much calmer frame of mind; instead of being furious, you can be 'curious' and, therefore, avoid being forced to adopt a position where you have to discipline in any punishing manner. When you adopt such an approach, there will be a positive impact on your own level of calmness, and this can also help to build up a sense of trust between you and the child or young person you are supporting.

The steps involved in emotion coaching are:

1. Be aware of the child's emotion.

2. Take the opportunity to connect.

3. Listen, empathize and validate.

4. Label the emotion.

5. Set limits, problem-solve and repair.

REFLECTION POINT
What emotions could be underlying these behaviours:

- hitting another child

- stealing from another student

- swearing at staff

- playing truant

- disrupting a lesson

- refusing to complete the work in class?

Top tips and strategies

It is very important to take some time now to gain a deeper under-standing of the emotion coaching process and consider how you might use the stepped approach below in your interactions with children and young people you support.

Before you can effectively emotion coach, you must first *understand your own approach to emotions*. Some school staff, for example, feel very uncomfortable when children or young people cry in front of them or show that they are feeling highly anxious or vulnerable. This means that if a child feels sad, the member of staff might feel a need to fix the problem for them as quickly as possible to make the crying stop. Someone else may find that a child's anger makes them feel angry and defensive too, leading them to discipline the child for feeling angry, when that is a normal and natural emotion; in essence, they will be punishing a child for showing symptoms of anxiety, fear or distress. Reflecting on this, you can see how illogical and damaging it could be.

REFLECTION POINT

At the outset, it's crucial to identify how you tend to respond to your own big or strong emotions, as well as those of the children and young people you are working with. This level of self-knowledge is essential in developing your ability to manage these emotional moments.

Gottman & DeClaire (1997) suggest several questions to think about to explore your own emotional awareness:

1. Did your parents treat sad, angry or fearful moments as being normal and natural?

2. Did your parents listen, validate and empathize when family members felt unhappy, fearful or angry?

3. Did your parents use times of emotional distress to connect, support and help each other solve problems?

4. Was anger seen as a negative, destructive emotion? Were you punished for experiencing anger? If so, what did this teach you about how to handle your anger?

5. Was fear looked on as cowardly? If so, how did you learn to handle fear?

6. Was sadness seen as self-pity in your family? In what ways were you taught to handle sadness?

7. Were sadness, anger and fear shoved under the blanket or dismissed as unproductive, naughty or self-indulgent?

Take some time to answer these questions and discuss them with a colleague or friend. This may help you make sense of your responses to strong or big emotions – both in yourself and others.

The stepped approach

Step 1: Be aware of the child's emotion

As explained previously, the emotion underneath the surface may not be immediately apparent from the behaviour being displayed. For example, a child may be displaying aggressive and 'angry' behaviours when they are actually in 'fight-or-flight' mode, experiencing anxiety or shame. Try to take a metaphorical step back and look at the situation with curiosity to try to understand how the child might be feeling.

Step 2: Believe that the child's emotions are an opportunity for connection and teaching

Using logic to reason away a child's emotions is rarely successful and often results in a confrontation. Validation, acceptance and empathy provide connection and allow for trust and safety to develop within the relationship.

Step 3: Listen with empathy and understanding, then validate the child's feelings

If you really want to understand a child or young person, you have to be able to put yourself in their shoes and try to feel what they are feeling. This kind of empathetic listening underpins the emotion coaching approach. We have to show empathy to our children before we can begin to develop or propose solutions with them or for them.

So, what does this kind of listening look like? Gottman & DeClaire (1997) suggests that empathetic listeners do the following:

- use their eyes to identify physical evidence of the child's emotions

- use their ears to hear the underlying messages behind what a child is saying

- use their imaginations to put themselves in the child's shoes to understand how they're feeling

- use words to reflect back what they hear, see, and imagine in a soothing, non-judgemental way, which also helps the child label the emotion

- use their hearts to feel what the child is feeling.

Once the child or young person feels understood, you can reassure them that their feelings are okay. It is pretty normal, and you are not dismissing it. What may not be okay is their behaviour. In other words, their feelings are always okay, even if their actions are not.

Step 4: Label the child's emotions

What are they actually feeling? They don't always have the emotional vocabulary needed to put their feelings into words. This results in their emotions being shown through their behaviours. In their book *The Whole-Brain Child*, Dr Dan Siegel and Dr Tina Payne Bryson advocate an approach called 'Name It to Tame It', in which the adult supports the child by labelling the emotion.

Putting a verbal label on the emotion helps the child feel understood and provides validation for their feelings. Research shows that labelling an emotion reduces the intensity of the emotion, and the child feels more connected to the adult (Torre & Lieberman, 2018). For example, suppose you observe aloud that the child seems 'angry' or 'sad' or 'disappointed'. In that case, you can help the child or young person change an overwhelming, uncomfortable feeling into something that feels more manageable.

An opportunity to label an emotion will frequently arise when listening actively with empathy (see Chapter 3 for more on this). It is essential to remain vigilant at this point, as it can be tempting to tell the child or young person how they ought to be feeling, rather than relating to what they are actually feeling at that given point in time.

For example, five-year-old Josh shouts that he hates his friend Marcus because Marcus took his toy. While it could be tempting in this situation to dwell on telling Josh that 'hate' is a strong word and that he doesn't really mean that, the adult validates his feelings and labels the emotion by saying, 'It sounds like you're quite angry that Marcus took your toy'.

Step 5: Set boundaries and problem-solve

This part of the process must occur once the child is calm and, therefore, able to use logic and be rational about the situation. It's essential to allow enough time for this process of calming, or self-regulation, to take place. Gottman & DeClaire (1997) describe several parts to this step:

- *Limit setting* – While accepting and validating the child's feelings is important, their actions may not have been acceptable. Once we set a limit on inappropriate behaviour and its consequences, we can follow through and be consistent. For example, the adult might say, 'You're angry that Marcus took that toy from you. I would be angry, too, if someone took something of mine without asking. But it is never okay to shout at someone that you hate them.'

- *Identifying goals* – In some cases, it may be appropriate to use a natural consequence for the inappropriate behaviour (e.g. not getting the toy back to demonstrate that shouting unkind words was not a good strategy to achieve the end goal). We can then talk to the child to identify, from their perspective, the goal they were trying to reach with their behaviour (e.g. getting Marcus to return the toy).

- *Problem-solving to explore possible solutions* – Give the child an opportunity to think up solutions to a problematic situation before you offer suggestions. This helps the child develop problem-solving skills. Try not to immediately dismiss their solutions if they're not workable. Instead, ask questions that will help them to see the outcome of their solutions. For example:
    - 'Is this solution fair?'
    - 'Will this solution work?'
    - 'Is it safe?'
    - 'How are you likely to feel? How are other people likely to feel?'

- *Helping the child choose a solution* – It is important to enable the child or young person to learn by seeing the consequences of their choices. If a solution doesn't seem to be working, that is okay; but it means that it may need some reworking, and you can therefore help the child or young person to come up with a more appropriate plan of action so that the solution is actually achievable.

Questions and prompts

It can often be helpful to develop a series of scripts, key phrases or prompts that you can use to support you in the process of emotion coaching with children and young people. In the initial stages, the phrases or questions in Table 5.2 can be helpful to guide you. However, over time, these will become more automatic, and you will develop a more natural way of responding and interacting with children and young people.

Table 5.2 Helpful questions and prompts

Step 3: Empathizing and validating	'I see...' or 'I notice...' 'I hear...' 'I'm wondering...' 'Tell me about that...' 'Are you saying that...' 'It's okay to feel that way.' 'I would feel angry too if I felt something was unfair.' 'It's normal to feel that way sometimes.'
Step 4: Labelling emotions	'Are you feeling...?' 'Is there anything else that you are feeling?' 'I imagine that feels...' 'It sounds to me like you feel... because... Is that right?' 'How does that make you feel?'
Step 5: Setting limits	'It's okay to feel..., but it's never okay to...' 'Even when we are annoyed, we can't act in that way because it's not safe.' 'This isn't a safe place to be angry – let's go somewhere safe, and then we can talk.'
Step 5 continued: Problem-solving	'Tell me what happened to make you feel this way.' 'What can you do to solve this problem?' 'Can you remember feeling this way before and what you did?' 'How did you handle it last time?' 'What could you do differently next time you feel this way?' 'Is there anyone that could help you with this?' 'Let's take a look at some different choices...'

CASE STUDY
Example script
After getting down to Cameron's level...

'I can see your head on the desk, and I'm wondering if you might be feeling stressed and overwhelmed by this work because it looks really hard. Am I right? Is there anything else that you're feeling?

It's normal to feel overwhelmed sometimes, especially when you're tired and you're having a bad day. My emotions feel much harder to manage when I'm tired, too. It's okay to feel stressed and frustrated, but it's not okay to throw your work on the floor.

Do you want to take a few moments to calm down, and then we can talk about what might help?'

Once calm...

'What were you trying to achieve by throwing the paper on the floor and putting your head on the desk? What did you need in that moment? How else could you have signalled to the teacher that you weren't feeling ready to learn? What could you do differently next time you feel this way? How can you make the situation right this time?'

Outcome...
Cameron picked up the piece of paper and apologized to his teacher. They discussed the stress that had been building up and ways that it could be reduced. He suggested that he avoid certain friends at break time who frequently wind him up. Cameron confided in the member of staff about his mum's illness and agreed that it might be helpful for teachers to know about the stress that he is under so that they can support him better. He also agreed for her to look into additional support for him as a young carer. Cameron suggested that, while he didn't want to have to tell his teacher if he needed to take a moment to calm down, he would like to have a subtle signal so that he could take a few minutes outside alone when needed, and another subtle signal to tell an adult that he needs help. He identified a peer he would like to sit next to, to whom he feels he can also turn for help.

Key points to remember when using emotion coaching

- The child's feelings are important.

- The child's feelings and wishes are okay, even if their actions aren't.

- Experiencing negative emotions, such as sadness, anger or fear, is important.

- Negative feelings are a chance for connection.

- Understanding what causes the child's feelings is important.

- Negative feelings are an opportunity for problem-solving.

- Negative feelings can be an opportunity for learning.

REFLECTION POINT

Think about your own skills in emotion coaching and try to answer the following questions:

1. What aspects of emotion coaching do you think you already apply in your role?

2. Can you see how emotion coaching might be applied in your practice?

3. Can you think of an incident when emotion coaching could have been used?

4. Can you see any possible challenges?

5. How could these be overcome?

References

Goleman, D. (1995) *Emotional Intelligence*. New York, NY: Bantam Books.

Gottman, J. & DeClaire, J. (1997) *Raising an Emotionally Intelligent Child*. Hoboken, NJ: Prentice Hall.

Siegel, D. & Bryson, T.P. (2012) *The Whole-Brain Child: 12 Revolutionary Strategies to Nurture Your Child's Developing Mind*. London: Robinson.

Torre, J.B. & Lieberman, M.D. (2018) 'Putting feelings into words: Affect labeling as implicit emotion regulation.' *Emotion Review, 10*(2), 116–124. doi:10.1177/1754073917742706

CHAPTER 6

Understanding Anxiety

What is anxiety?

Anxiety is a normal, useful and natural response to a perceived threat. Anxiety evokes physical, emotional and mental responses, including an increase in adrenaline, feelings of worry and confusion, and thoughts about danger and catastrophic outcomes. Normal levels of anxiety can actually help people to be more focused and motivated, and to solve problems more efficiently. However, long-term or high levels of anxiety can reduce a person's capacity to respond effectively to stressful situations. For example, a highly anxious person may experience constant physical feelings of panic and may seek to avoid anything that might trigger their anxiety (such as using public transport, going to school or talking in front of others).

Anxiety can be triggered by many different situations. Sources of anxiety may include (but are not limited to) fear of:

- social situations

- speaking, eating or writing in front of other people

- negative evaluation and rejection

- performing in front of others

- a specific object or situation (e.g. sickness, lightning/thunder, insects, blood)

- separation from a parent/carer

- a parent/carer being harmed

- injury to oneself

- academic performance and exams

- starting school or work

- the future (what will happen, how it might turn out).

Anxiety may manifest itself in physical symptoms such as muscle tension, trembling, nausea, faster breathing, increased heart rate, sweating, blushing or feeling hot or cold. In addition, children and young people experiencing anxiety may display a number of behavioural symptoms, including withdrawing from friends and family, leaving the classroom frequently and avoidance of particular situations.

When the anxiety experienced by a young person starts to affect their general functioning, they may not just be feeling stressed – they may be experiencing an *anxiety disorder*. Anxiety disorders are one of the most common types of mental health concerns for children and young people.

'I was diagnosed with an anxiety disorder myself and have had to learn strategies to cope. I think this has actually really helped me to support children because I notice little signs that others might miss if they hadn't experienced it themselves. For a long time, I hated and feared my anxiety, but now I see it as my superpower!' (Katie, teacher)

The anxiety disorders include:

- *Generalized anxiety disorder (GAD)* – Excessive and persistent anxiety about events and activities related to work, study, health, finances, family issues or other general concerns. People who have GAD have difficulty controlling worry and the associated physical and emotional symptoms, such as restlessness, fatigue, difficulties in concentrating, muscle tension and sleep disturbance. GAD affects approximately 6 percent of people (Kessler et al., 2005).

- *Panic attacks and panic disorder* – Panic attacks are the term used to describe the sudden onset of severe physical and cognitive symptoms of anxiety. A panic attack can include shortness of breath, accelerated heart rate, trembling, sweating, dizziness and fear of going crazy or dying. Fear of panic attacks in public places may lead to agoraphobia. Panic disorder is the name used to describe recurrent and unexpected panic attacks and persistent concerns of repeated attacks. Panic disorder affects approximately 5 percent of people (Kessler et al., 2005).

- *Obsessive compulsive disorder (OCD)* – OCD is the term for recurrent and persistent intrusive thoughts (obsessions), and repetitive ritualistic behaviours (compulsions). For example, fear of contamination or harm to self or others, leading to excessive hand-washing, showering and checking or repeating routine actions. OCD affects about 2 percent of people (Kessler et al., 2005).

- *Post-traumatic stress disorder (PTSD)* – PTSD may develop following exposure to a distressing and traumatic event or ongoing traumatic situation. Recurrent thoughts, images and nightmares of the trauma occur, as well as mood changes. Other symptoms include emotional reactivity, memory and concentration difficulties. Around 7 percent of people are affected by PTSD (Kessler et al., 2005).

- *Social phobia* – This is the anticipatory worry and avoidance of social and performance situations, due to fears of scrutiny and judgement by others, and fear of feeling humiliated or embarrassed in front of others. This may include speaking, eating or even writing in front of others. Social anxiety affects approximately 12 percent of people at some point in their lives, making it one of the most common anxiety disorders (Kessler et al., 2005).

- *Specific phobia(s)* – This refers to the excessive fear of a particular thing or type of situation. Phobias can start at any age, and a person may have more than one phobia. Specific phobias are estimated to affect approximately 7 percent of people at some point in their lives (Eaton et al., 2018). Common phobias include:

  - claustrophobia, or fear of small spaces such as fitting rooms

  - zoophobia, or fear of animals

  - acrophobia, or fear of heights, such as when flying

  - emetophobia, or fear of vomiting.

What is the purpose of anxiety?

When we perceive there to be a threat, this triggers a chain reaction in the body, commonly referred to as the 'fight-or-flight' response. This response has evolved because it was very useful to our cave person ancestors: those who were hypervigilant to possible threats around them and became anxious in the face of danger were at an evolutionary advantage. Simply put, those who were able to fight or run away from a dangerous situation successfully, were more likely to survive than those who responded in a more relaxed way. Therefore, anxiety is a normal, natural emotion that is there to keep us safe.

However, unfortunately, the fight-or-flight response isn't so helpful when responding to modern-day stress factors like bills, exams, relationship difficulties and looking after our families. Our brains are also not so good at distinguishing between a real threat and one that is imagined. For example, we might watch a horror film knowing it isn't real, yet we still become anxious.

What happens in our bodies when we are anxious?

When the brain's fear centre (the amygdala) recognizes a potential threat (e.g. a spider, a social situation, an exam), a distress signal is sent to the hypothalamus, sometimes referred to as our brain's 'control centre'. It is this part of the brain that communicates with the rest of the body, through the autonomic nervous system, to help keep the body in balance, regulating our heartbeat, breathing, body temperature, and so on. The autonomic nervous system has two branches: the sympathetic and parasympathetic branches. The sympathetic branch is likened to the accelerator pedal on a car: it gets the body revved up to respond quickly. In contrast, the parasympathetic branch is like the body's brake pedal: it calms the body down to return to a relaxed state.

As you might have guessed, anxiety – or the fight-or-flight response – happens when the sympathetic branch of the autonomic nervous system is activated. This results in adrenaline being released, as well as glucose, which gives us a sudden energy boost to fight against a predator or run away from danger. Our pupils dilate to allow us to take in more visual information from our environment, and functions that aren't necessary for responding to danger shut down, including our digestive systems, meaning that we may experience a dry mouth, lump in the throat, butterflies, nausea and loss of appetite. Our heart rate increases to pump blood to our muscles more quickly, and our breathing becomes more rapid, allowing us to take in as much oxygen as possible with each breath.

Our brains also feel the effects of this response. For example, according to Goleman (1995), our pre-frontal cortex – which is responsible for reasoning, logic, planning and memory – gets overridden by the amygdala. Goleman coined the term 'amygdala hijack' to describe this. This process allows us to respond quickly and impulsively in the face of danger, without overthinking. This is very useful if we need to quickly leap into action when a sabre-tooth tiger is charging towards us, but less so when we find ourselves in an interview or exam and our 'mind goes blank'!

> *'I explained the fight-or-flight response to a child in Year 4, and the response was incredible. It was like a light switch went on and he suddenly understood that all of the terrifying feelings that he had been experiencing in his body were normal and useful and not a sign that he was dying!' (Roisin, teaching assistant)*

REFLECTION POINT

Stop and think about a time when you have felt a heightened level of anxiety. What did this feel like in your body and how did it affect your feelings and ability to concentrate on a task? Why do you think it is so important to be able to support children and young people who exhibit anxiety? What would you advise right now? Do you feel that you need to develop your skills so that you can co-regulate with them?

What does anxiety look like?

It may be that you can spot some of the more obvious physical symptoms of the stress response, including faster breathing, shaking and sweating. However, anxiety can often be difficult to identify in oneself and in others because the symptoms feel so physical. Sometimes, for adults, it can be challenging to recognize, for example, a headache, nausea or sweating as signs of anxiety, as they can feel so similar to physical illness.

For a child who has less experience with feelings of anxiety, and who does not have the vocabulary to place a label on the feelings that they are experiencing, we need to be able to recognize more subtle behaviours that may indicate anxiety.

- Physical symptoms to look out for:
  - fast breathing
  - rapid heartbeat
  - trembling
  - tension in muscles (e.g. fists clenched, shoulders hunched, appearance rigid)
  - nausea/vomiting/stomach-aches
  - headaches
  - frequently feeling unwell
  - flushing
  - sweating
  - dry mouth
- Behaviours to look out for:
  - avoidance (e.g. of school, lessons, assemblies, any situations that evoke fear)
  - sudden anger
  - urges to escape (e.g. leaving the classroom frequently or without warning, wanting to ensure an escape route, such as by sitting on the end of a row in assembly)
  - frequent toilet trips
  - difficulty sleeping
  - lack of focus
  - defiance and controlling behaviour (to avoid feelings of helplessness)

- overplanning (to gain control and feelings of safety)
- big reactions to small situations
- perfectionism
- restlessness
- difficulty coping with change
- often complaining of physical illness
- regression
- tics, noises and repetitive movements
- zoning out
- Language to look out for:
  - frequent checking and need for reassurance
  - voicing irrational and excessive fear
  - negative self-talk
  - catastrophizing (expecting the worst to happen)
  - mind-reading (e.g. thinking that others think negatively about them)
  - 'what ifs' (using negative phrases beginning with the words 'what if' are often an indicator of anxiety).

REFLECTION POINT
Think about a child you think may have anxiety. Tick which of the above signs and symptoms you have noticed in them.

CASE STUDY
Tao is in Year 4. He hates coming to school and often lashes out at members of staff who are involved in trying to get him in. He shouts, hits, kicks and doesn't seem to care that he hurts members of staff and children. When they can get him into school, he often runs from

the classroom when no one is looking. Staff are at the end of their tether with him. Some staff members are scared of him because he can be so aggressive towards everyone; but at other times, he is kind and gentle. In the staffroom, a member of staff went as far as to call him a 'psychopath' because he is so unpredictable and volatile. Last week, Tao pushed away a member of staff who was trying to get him into class in the morning. She fell backwards and now Tao has been given a temporary exclusion for violent and aggressive behaviour.

Questions

1. Why might Tao be reluctant to come to school in the morning?

2. How could the hitting, kicking and pushing be better understood?

3. What is the purpose of this behaviour for Tao?

4. Why do you think that Tao's behaviour seems unpredictable?

5. What approach or strategies do you think might be best to reduce the physical outbursts that Tao is exhibiting in the mornings?

It sounds as though Tao is exhibiting behaviours that are consistent with the fight-or-flight response. In the mornings, he is so anxious about coming into school that when staff approach him and try to coax him into the classroom, he reacts in a physical way to fight the perceived threat (school). During the school day, he sometimes experiences an overwhelming need to escape from the stressful situation and frequently leaves the classroom. In this case, his behaviour has been incorrectly assumed by some staff to be malicious, manipulative and aggressive, leading to harmful and cruel gossip in the staffroom. Unfortunately, in this situation, because Tao's needs were not understood, staff took a very firm and assertive approach to getting him into school. This exacerbated his anxiety and resulted in a member of staff being hurt. It is likely that working with Tao to reduce his anxiety would have been a more successful approach to changing the behaviours they were seeing.

Individual differences in anxiety

Anxiety describes a very normal and natural emotion that we feel in response to situations that feel stressful to us. These reactions vary enormously between people and heavily depend on how we think about different situations. For example, when faced with a spider, some people will think, 'Yikes! That spider will run towards me and try to crawl up my leg!' If that is the thought process, the resulting feelings will be anxiety, fear and dread. The actions that are likely to follow are screaming and running away or avoiding the spider. This avoidance relieves the anxiety in the short term and reinforces the message that we were only safe in that situation because we managed to escape, which means that the negative thoughts about spiders are confirmed and continue.

However, if on seeing a spider your thoughts are more along the lines of, 'Oh, a spider. It can't harm me – I am much more of a threat to it than it is to me', then your feelings and behaviour will follow a different path. Your feelings are likely to be less notable, and your actions may be just to ignore the spider and carry on with your day, or to put it safely outside.

This example illustrates the importance of our thought process and its impact on our feelings and behaviours. This cycle of thoughts, feelings and behaviours forms the basis of cognitive behavioural therapy (CBT), which is one of the most effective approaches for reducing anxiety. We will discuss ways in which you can use this approach later on in this chapter, and in more detail in Chapter 7.

What is the difference between anxiety and an anxiety disorder?

As we have repeated throughout this chapter, anxiety is a normal and useful emotion that has evolved to keep us safe. It is important, therefore, that this common human experience is not pathologized unnecessarily. Children and young people need to know that if they feel a bit anxious about, for example, an exam, standing up in assembly or performing in front of others, it does not mean something is wrong with them! However, frequent feelings of anxiety can also be a sign of an anxiety disorder, which may require some additional support. *While this can only be diagnosed by a medical professional*, anxiety disorders tend to be characterized by anxiety that is more severe and long-lasting and impacts on the person's ability to function at home, in school or socially.

'Young people look at social media and think everyone is happy and living their best life all the time. It's so misleading! It means that when they feel anxious about something, or have a down day, they think there must be something wrong with them.' (Justine, secondary school teacher)

Top tips and strategies
FIRES

The FIRES Framework that was introduced in Chapter 1 can guide you to support you in responding effectively in situations where you are concerned that a young person is feeling anxious. A full description of the framework is given in Chapter 1, so it is important to read that first, but here is a reminder of the steps...

- **F**ast response

- **I**dentify needs and risks

- **R**eassure

- **E**mpathize and listen

- **S**upport and signpost

Support and signpost

After all of the other very important steps (and only after!) you can move to supporting and signposting.

- *Support them to challenge underlying beliefs and thoughts* – Negative and irrational beliefs and thoughts such as 'If I don't look perfect, no one will like me' or 'I can't cope with difficult or scary situations', are significant factors in generating anxiety. Model and communicate effective ways to question and challenge anxiety-provoking thoughts and beliefs. For example, 'What would you say to a friend who had that thought?' or 'What might your friend say to you if they knew that you were thinking that way?'

- *Be patient* – Sometimes, the behaviours of anxious children and young people may seem unreasonable to others. It is important to remember that an anxious young person who cries or avoids situations is responding instinctively to a perceived threat. Changing avoidant behaviours takes time and persistence.

- *Show children and young people some simple relaxation techniques* – Breathing activities, progressive muscle relaxation and mindfulness can be helpful as ways of learning how to manage physical anxiety symptoms better. Generally, these techniques are most effective if practised consistently over several weeks.

- *Encourage plenty of physical exercise and appropriate amounts of sleep* – When people are well-rested, they will be better able to regulate feelings of anxiety.

- *Discourage consumption of caffeine and high-sugar products* – Caffeine products, including cola and energy drinks, increase levels of anxiety as they cause energy levels to spike and then crash. This leaves a person feeling drained and less able to deal with negative thoughts. Caffeine also increases activity in the sympathetic branch of the autonomic nervous system, meaning that the effects on the body can feel very similar to those induced by the stress response.

- *Make time for things that the child enjoys and finds relaxing* – These could be simple things, like playing or listening to music, reading a book or walking in nature.

- *Help them to face the things or situations they fear* – Learning to face their fears and reduce avoidance of feared objects and situations is one of the most challenging parts of overcoming anxiety. Facing fears usually works best if undertaken gradually, one step at a time.

- *Encourage help-seeking when needed* – Make sure that children and young people know there are people who can help if they find that they can't handle a problem on their own. Knowing that they can call on others for support if needed will make them feel less anxious about what might happen in the future.

- *Support them to accept uncertainty* – Uncertainty is one thing that people worry about a lot, because of the potential for negative outcomes. As it is impossible to eliminate uncertainty, you can assist children and young people to be more accepting of uncertainty and ambiguity.

- *Be a role model* – If you can regulate your own anxiety, young people will see that it can be managed and might incorporate your strategies into their own behaviours. Teaching parents to manage their own anxiety has been shown to be helpful in reducing their children's anxiety.

- *Work with the parents* – Speak to the parents about their views and concerns. Working together and using consistent strategies will give the best chance of success.

- *Work with teachers and other school staff* – You may need to act as an advocate for the child, as fear often produces extremely antisocial behaviour. You will learn what has been tried and how the problem is viewed. Do not condemn staff at school for lack of understanding. Ensure that you inform the mental health lead and designated safeguarding lead about your concerns if they are not aware that the young person may be struggling with their anxiety.

Top phrases to use to support and calm

- 'I'm here with you.'

- 'These feelings will pass.'

- 'You are safe.'

- 'You've been through this before, and you can do it again.'

- 'This must be so hard for you.'

- 'It's okay to feel anxious.'

- 'I can see you are worried – what can I do to help?'

Anxiety ladder

You can help children to face their fears using the 'anxiety ladder'. This involves working out as many gentle steps as possible to build up exposure to the feared thing. For example, if a child is afraid of dogs, a ladder may begin with hearing about a dog or looking at a picture of one. You can draw a ladder with ten or more steps and then write down all of the gentle, easy steps for the child to gradually face in order to conquer their fear. You can write a step on each rung. Begin with the easiest rung on the ladder and build up very, very slowly, noticing and celebrating every step of the way. Practise relaxation strategies while the child or young person takes the step, to help them to cope and learn to associate their feared situation with feeling calm and in control. As you continue over time, the young person will build up good evidence that it is okay to be with the feared object or situation, and that fears do not have to be there for ever.

Anxiety support plan

Intense feelings of anxiety can make it difficult to think clearly. Making a proactive plan with the child or young person when they are feeling calm can help to empower them with strategies to use in the moment. The suggested prompts in the handout use a cognitive behavioural approach to help them to recognize their triggers, physiological symptoms, thoughts, support system and self-help strategies.

Anxiety Ladder

Situation: ....

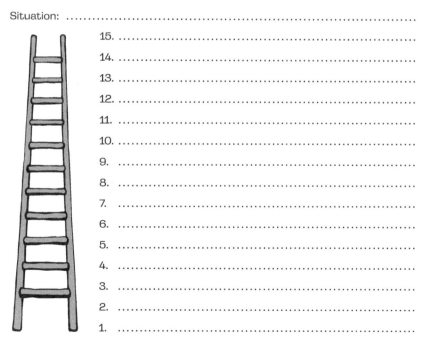

15. ....
14. ....
13. ....
12. ....
11. ....
10. ....
9. ....
8. ....
7. ....
6. ....
5. ....
4. ....
3. ....
2. ....
1. ....

✳ MY ANXIETY SUPPORT PLAN

What are the triggers for my anxiety?

How does my body feel when I am anxious?

What thoughts go through my head when I am anxious?

What positive thoughts can I think instead?

What helps when I start to feel anxious?

What can I do to support my wellbeing every day?

At school, I can talk to...

At home, I can talk to...

At 3 a.m., I can talk to...

When I am alone, I can talk to...

Apps, websites or phone lines that help me:

Planning ahead: A six-step approach

This six-step approach can develop into a lifelong skill, aiding pupils in effectively managing their stress now and in the future. Encourage pupils to use the following steps to guide them:

1. Envision the situation or event in detail (e.g. going into an exam hall), focusing on anticipated emotions. Practise slow, deep breathing during this visualization to start to relieve these feelings, and associate thinking about the event with feeling calm and in control.

2. Prepare for the situation or event. If you need more clarification about a specific topic for an upcoming exam, seek assistance by asking teachers, consulting friends or doing more revision.

3. Acknowledge and accept various possibilities (e.g. there might be questions that I cannot answer) and commit to maintaining calmness and relaxation in each scenario.

4. Create contingency plans. This diminishes the perceived threat of the situation or event. For instance, if tasked with presenting to a group and unsure of the script, have it written on memory cards for reference in case of a lapse.

5. Prioritize relaxation by allocating time before the event. Activities such as running, taking a bath or mindfulness can help.

6. Reward yourself and relax after the stressful situation or event. You deserve it!

References

Eaton, W.W., Bienvenu. O.J. & Miloyan, B. (2018) 'Specific phobias.' *Lancet Psychiatry,* 5(8), 678–686.

Goleman, D. (1995) *Emotional Intelligence.* New York, NY: Bantam Books.

Kessler, R.C., Berglund, P., Demler, O., Jin, R., Merikangas, K.R. & Walters, E.E. (2005) 'Lifetime prevalence and age-of-onset distributions of DSM-IV disorders in the National Comorbidity Survey Replication.' *Archives of General Psychiatry, 62*(6), 593–602.

CHAPTER 7

Supporting Those Who Self-harm

What is self-harm?

Self-harm means doing something to cause yourself harm or not doing something that in turn may cause harm (e.g. not taking prescribed medications or purposefully damaging an insulin pump). Some definitions of self-harm include the wording 'deliberate', which can be misleading, given that it implies that self-harm is a choice. Many young people feel that they have no choice or control over this behaviour and use it as a way to cope with their emotions. Self-harm includes behaviours such as:

- taking too many tablets

- burning

- cutting or scratching

- banging

- breaking own bones

- pulling own hair

- swallowing toxic substances or other inappropriate objects.

Self-harm remains a significant public health issue among young people in the United Kingdom, affecting at least one in 14 young people (McManus et al., 2016). Research suggests that girls are three times more likely to self-harm than boys, and self-harm is a significant risk factor for suicide (Morgan et al., 2017).

Despite concerns over the impact of the COVID-19 pandemic on the mental health and wellbeing of young people, the statistics suggest that there has not been an increase in self-harming behaviours during the pandemic. In fact, one study showed a significant decrease in reported self-harm (Carr et al., 2021). It was suggested that this may be due to reduced academic pressure, reduced bullying and increased contact with and support from parents. However, these findings may also be due to a reduction in the identification of self-harming, given that self-harming behaviours are almost by definition secretive, and parents and carers frequently will not know what is happening. The reduction in the reporting of self-harm may also be due to young people being less likely to seek medical treatment given the risks of contracting COVID-19 from hospitals.

The issue of self-harm in children and young people is probably one of the most challenging and complex areas for those in the school context to manage. Primarily, this is because most adults who have had little experience with such responses to psychological pain will find these behaviours difficult to understand and often very frightening to both witness and talk about. At the outset, many will feel nervous that they might be responding in an inappropriate or unhelpful way, and that what they say could do more damage than good.

What is important to remember is that, for many children and young people, self-harm has been normalized via social media and self-harm websites, and entering into such discussions may not be as traumatic for them as we think. It is vital that we always maintain a non-judgemental and empathic approach in our interactions: it takes a tremendous amount of courage for a young person to approach an adult to discuss self-harming behaviours, and our initial response is critical. If we respond with anger or disgust, they are unlikely to open up again or to seek the help that they may need for their mental health. Therefore, it is extremely important to understand why children and young people use self-harm as a means of managing psychological pain, and how to support those who do so in a safe and ethical manner in the school context.

> 'Miss Byers told me that sometimes, when people are feeling big emotions, they cope with them by harming themselves, and she asked me whether that was how I got the marks on my legs. I had tried so hard to hide it for so long, but, in that moment, it was actually a huge relief to finally talk about it to someone.' (Tara, student, aged 17)

Signs of self-harm

If a child or young person is self-harming, you may notice one or more of the following behaviours:

- changes in clothing, such as wearing long-sleeved tops in an attempt to cover up evidence of scarring or self-harm

- changes in eating or sleeping habits

- increased isolation from friends and family, or a reluctance to engage in the usual social activities

- changes in behaviour or mood, for example, presenting as more aggressive than usual

- decrease in engagement in terms of academic progress or development, including lowering grades or attainment levels

- talking about self-harming or suicide in an open manner

- abusing drugs or alcohol

- presenting as socially withdrawn

- expressing feelings of failure, uselessness or a loss of hope.

Myths around self-harm

It is crucial to understand that engaging in self-harming behaviours is not a calculated decision, contrary to what some may believe. Numerous misconceptions surround self-harm, with a prominent one being the idea that these actions are intended as a way of seeking attention. This notion is inaccurate and must be consistently challenged. Individuals who self-harm do so as a response to genuine distress and overwhelming emotional pain, using self-harm as a means of releasing that pain. While some may only self-harm occasionally, others develop a regular pattern, resembling an addiction.

Another misconception to dispel is that young people can simply stop self-harming if instructed to do so by a significant adult. This is not the case. The young person would likely have already done so if stopping self-harming were easily achievable. To add to this, young people often go to great lengths to hide their self-harm from adults. Some may open up to a trusted adult at school but resist disclosing such information to parents or caregivers, making it even more difficult for adults to intervene successfully.

REFLECTION POINT

Think about self-harm in relation to yourself. Many people will have had some experience with this issue. You may find it helpful to ask yourself if you understand the need to dispel these myths. Also, think about what you may currently be doing that is potentially unhealthy – for example, over or undereating, drinking too much alcohol, maintaining an unhealthy relationship. Who can or do you talk to for support?

Then think about how you would respond right now if a child or young person disclosed their self-harming to you. What would you say and do? What systems are in place to support you?

It might be useful to write out a helpful, non-judgemental script and share this with colleagues.

The cycle of self-harm

Self-harm can be viewed as a cycle (Sutton, 2009). Negative thoughts lead to uncomfortable emotions and a drive to find a release. In some people, this can trigger an act of self-harm, which is positively reinforced through the release of endorphins, leading to a short-term reduction in stress and improvement in mood. However, in the long term, the negative emotions and thought processes remain and can be worsened through the regret, guilt and shame triggered by the self-harming act. For those supporting children and young people, the idea is to be able to intercept the cycle by challenging the negative thoughts and emotions that trigger the need to self-harm. Using tools from CBT is very often helpful to children and young people who are trapped in this cycle.

Top tips and strategies
Challenging negative automatic thoughts (NATs) using tools from CBT

CBT is based on the premise that how we think can affect how we feel and behave. For example, if you interpret a situation negatively (e.g. the spider that we referred to in Chapter 6), this might result in negative emotions, and those negative feelings might then lead you to behave in a certain way. Figure 7.1 shows how this creates a vicious cycle of worry and avoidance.

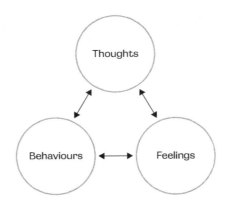

FIGURE 7.1 VICIOUS CYCLE OF WORRY AND AVOIDANCE

How does CBT work?

CBT aims to identify and challenge any negative thinking patterns and behaviour that may be causing the anxiety. By challenging our thinking, we can change how we feel about situations and how we behave in the future. CBT involves structured learning experiences that teach people to notice and write down their negative automatic thoughts, for example, by keeping a thought diary. The goal is to recognize our own negative thinking and how those ideas affect our mood and behaviour, and to be able to challenge those thoughts. CBT also involves teaching important coping skills, such as problem-solving and self-care.

Table 7.1 shows some examples of common negative automatic thoughts to look out for. *The idea of CBT is to learn to recognize those negative thoughts and find a healthier way to view the situation.* Once the inaccuracy of the assumption becomes evident, the individual can replace that perspective with a more accurate one.

Table 7.1 Common negative thoughts

Negative automatic thought	What is it?	Example
All-or-nothing thinking	Thinking in extremes without anything in the middle	'I am the worst at...' or 'I never get anything right'
Overgeneralization	Thinking that one bad thing happening means that everything will always be that bad	'I failed my exam! I am destined to be a failure!'
Mental filter	Only focusing on the negative and ignoring the positive	Focusing on the one question that you got wrong, rather than all the ones that were right
Disqualifying the positive	Disbelieving positives or turning them into negatives	'They only said I did well because they pity me.'
Catastrophizing	Jumping to the worst-case scenario and overestimating the likelihood of that occurring	'I'll fail all of my exams, and my life will be ruined!'
Fortune-telling	Predicting future events in a negative way	'I'll always be anxious, and my life will be miserable.'
Mind-reading	Thinking that others are thinking negative things about you	'They all hate me and think I am stupid.'
Negative comparisons	Comparing yourself negatively to others	'Everyone else is happy and has it together. I am just a mess!'

CASE STUDY

Tara was 15 years old when Miss Byers, a teaching assistant, spoke to her about the marks she had noticed on her legs. Throughout a few meetings, Tara began to open up about how she had been feeling. Tara explained that she felt under too much pressure with her upcoming exams. She expressed that she felt like she was going to fail, and that everyone would be disappointed in her. She had been predicted all As, and that just seemed like an impossible feat, meaning that no matter how hard she worked, she would just let everyone down.

She felt as though she was going to explode with the stress and pressure, and burning herself gave her the sudden, instant release that she needed. However, she admitted that it never took away the real problem, and she ended up just feeling ashamed and in pain. Her wounds often got infected, and she hated how they looked. It also meant carrying around what she perceived as a big shameful secret, which felt like an even bigger burden on top of everything else.

Miss Byers noticed that Tara was having some negative automatic thoughts, which were resulting in a lot of the stress and anxiety that she was feeling. Miss Byers challenged some of these, particularly around the likelihood of 'failing' and the evidence that others would feel 'disappointed' or 'let down'. Through simple questioning, Tara was able to see that these thoughts were not facts and was able to formulate some more realistic thoughts that felt a lot less distressing, reducing her anxiety. She was able to recognize that she had done well in her mocks, had done lots of revision, and it was very unlikely that she would fail. She may not get all As, but she could see that this did not mean 'failure'. She also acknowledged that her family loved her and just wanted her to try her best.

Miss Byers also taught Tara some alternative coping strategies for when she felt too overwhelmed. Together, they created a 'safety plan', detailing the strategies that she could try and whom she could talk to. This allowed Tara to stop self-harming, and now, two years on, she is a student wellbeing ambassador, providing support to other students.

Questions

1. How would you feel if a student showed you a self-inflicted injury?

2. How would you ensure the student could not read those feelings on your face as you supported them?

3. What tools did Miss Byers use to support Tara?

4. Do you have any ideas for alternative coping strategies that might help a student who is self-harming to feel a 'release'?

More strategies for supporting the child or young person

FIRES

The FIRES Framework introduced in Chapter 1 can help you respond safely and effectively in situations where you are concerned that a young person may be self-harming. A full description of the framework is given in Chapter 1, so it is important to read that first, but Table 7.2 gives some more specific considerations for supporting pupils who self-harm.

Table 7.2 FIRES and self-harm

F	Fast response	Never ignore warning signs.
I	Identify needs and risks	Does the young person need medical attention? Could they be a suicide risk? Remove alcohol if present.
R	Reassure	Respond calmly, without showing shock, disapproval or disgust, even if the young person is showing you significant injuries that they have inflicted.
E	Empathize and listen	Remember to focus on the feelings rather than the injuries. It is important not to judge the intensity of the distress by the severity of the injury.
S	Support and signpost	Make a safety plan. Inform the DSL, MHL and parents where possible. MHL should use the THRIVE Framework (see Chapter 1) to plan support with the young person and seek support and advice from the local CAMHS.

Distraction techniques

When supporting a child or young person who is self-harming, it is important to provide them with less-damaging alternatives to these behaviours. The idea is to begin to make use of these strategies when the urge to self-harm becomes apparent, and, over time, to decrease the most-damaging self-harming behaviours. Using distraction techniques can be part of the young person's safety plan.

Some of the most popular tried-and-tested distraction techniques identified by the Mental Health Foundation and Camelot Foundation (2006) are as follows:

- using a red water-soluble felt-tip pen to mark instead of cutting

- hitting a punch bag to release anger and frustration

- rubbing ice against the wrist

- exercise

- making lots of noise (e.g. shouting or banging on something)

- writing negative feelings on paper and then destroying it

- scribbling on paper with a red pen

- putting elastic bands on wrists and pinging

- expressing emotions in a diary or journal

- listening to songs that express how you feel

- talking to a friend about how you are feeling

- making a collage or mood board.

Key dos and don'ts
Do:

- *Stay calm* – Do not show anxiety, disapproval or disgust. Be prepared to be shocked, then... listen. Just being listened to can be a brilliant support and allows the person to relieve some of their feelings in a healthier way than self-harming.

- *Listen* – This does not just require ears: observe the young person's nonverbal clues; look at their body language. Does what they say and what you see match up? What is the underlying mood state? Is it anger? Sadness? Frustration?

- *Empathize* – Calmly ask any relevant questions; try and build rapport with the young person, while you ascertain what is happening for them. Remember, many young people may not understand what has led them to self-harm.

- *Remember the focus* – The primary concern is the young person's feelings rather than their injuries.

- *Think carefully before you act* – What is in the young person's best interest? Most episodes of self-harm have nothing to do with suicide, but the most effective way to differentiate between suicidal behaviour and self-harm is to ask the young person about the intentions behind the self-harming behaviours.

- *Treat a suicide intention as an emergency.* Do not leave the young person alone or in a vulnerable environment. Get help and support as soon as possible and remain calm.

Do not:

- *Panic* – Unfortunately, many young people self-harm; it is a complex issue, and each young person will have a different story or reason behind their behaviour. Panicking will not help the young person to feel safe and contained.

- *Send the young person away* – Make some time for them; either help them find other ways of coping or help them get the right kind of support.

- *Be judgemental* – Keep an open mind about the behaviour and do not refer to it as 'attention-seeking'.

- *Automatically try to stop the young person from self-harming* – This behaviour may be their only way of managing often powerful and painful feelings.

- *Work alone* – You may still see a young person alone, but you will need to offload with an appropriate staff member or colleague from another agency.

- *Offer to take the young person to your home environment* – Do not give them your mobile number or house number or get into the habit of texting the young person. It is more appropriate and professional to help the young person identify their own supportive network than for you to take this on yourself.

'A young person told me about his self-harming and showed me where he had cut himself. I'm really not good with blood and things like that, but I knew that if he could see shock or disgust in my face, he would shut down and never open up again.' (Adrian, teacher)

The importance of making a safety plan

A plan is essential for keeping the child or young person safe, both in and outside the school context, and for supporting them in their goal of reducing these behaviours over time. The following key points need to be observed when you are constructing a plan with the child or young person and their family:

- Do not just focus on telling them to stop, as this is counter-productive.

- Encourage them to keep talking about their feelings.

- Always list people they can go to for help at different times of the day; for example, whom can they turn to when they are in school, at the weekend or at 3 a.m.?

- Support them in making a 'safe box' or 'calm box', which includes a range of distracting activities and things that make them happy, or support them in relaxing when they feel the urge to engage in self-harming behaviours.

- Encourage them to try to avoid drugs and alcohol.

- Encourage them to maintain good sleeping habits.

- Share a range of self-help apps, such as 'Calm Harm' and 'Self-heal', that can help them alongside other forms of support.

See page 139 for a suggested format for a safety plan. It is a photocopiable resource, or you may wish to consider adapting or personalizing it for an individual child or young person.

✳ MY SAFETY PLAN

What makes me want to harm myself? For example, it could be particular people, feelings, places or memories.

Other than harming myself, what else can I do that helps me to cope?

What would I tell a close friend to do who was feeling this way?

What could others do that would help?

If I feel like harming myself again, I will do one of the following (try to list six items):

1. ....
2. ....
3. ....
4. ....
5. ....
6. ....

If the plan does not work and I still feel like harming myself, I will do at least one of the following:

Call Samaritans on 116 123

Call Childline on 0800 1111

Talk to a trusted adult [.........................]

Call emergency services on 999, or go to nearest A&E

Signed: .... Date: ....

References

Carr, M.J., Steeg, S., Webb, R.T., Kapur, N. et al. (2021) 'Effects of the COVID-19 pandemic on primary care-recorded mental illness and self-harm episodes in the UK: A population-based cohort study.' *Lancet Public Health, 6*(2), 124–135.

McManus S., Bebbington P., Jenkins R. & Brugha T. (Eds.) (2016) Adult Psychiatric Morbidity Survey: Survey of Mental Health and Wellbeing, England, 2014. https://webarchive.nationalarchives.gov.uk/ukgwa/20180328140249/http:/digital.nhs.uk/catalogue/PUB21748

Mental Health Foundation and Camelot Foundation (2006) *Truth Hurts: Report on the National Inquiry into Self-harm Among Young People.* London: Mental Health Foundation.

Morgan, C., Webb, R.T., Carr, M.J., Kontopantelis, E. et al. (2017) 'Incidence, clinical management, and mortality risk following self harm among children and adolescents: Cohort study in primary care.' *British Medical Journal, 359*, j4351.

Sutton, J. (2009) *Healing the Hurt Within.* Oxford: How To Books.

CHAPTER 8

Supporting Those with Panic Attacks

What is a panic attack?

A panic attack is the sudden onset of intense anxiety symptoms, such as a racing heart, shortness of breath and shaking, accompanied by a feeling of impending doom. The exact cause is unknown, but it is thought that genetics, stress and changes in brain function can all play a role.

Panic attacks begin suddenly, often without warning, but are short-lived, with *most panic attacks lasting up to 20 minutes*. They can strike at any time and may occur as occasional or frequent attacks. Symptoms include:

- fear of loss of control

- fear of impending doom

- flashing vision

- hyperventilation

- palpitations

- breathlessness

- chest pain

- sweating

- shaking

- headache

- chills

- nausea

- abdominal cramps

- dizzy feeling

- numbness

- suicidal ideation

- feeling faint

- feeling sweaty

- feeling weak or shaky in the legs

- fast heartbeat, or sense that the heart isn't beating normally

- sensation of choking or being unable to breathe easily

- blurry vision

- feeling strange or disconnected from surroundings.

'My panic attacks started when I was about ten years old after I had been off school with an ear infection. I felt sick every morning, and my parents had no idea what was wrong with me. I couldn't eat much because I felt sick with anxiety, and I remember my parents being concerned that I had an eating disorder. I felt completely out of control and panicked about panicking, meaning that if I had a panic attack at a certain place, I then worried about having a panic attack in that place again, meaning that it inevitably happened again and again. I ended up terrified of going to school, being out anywhere to eat, public transport, anywhere hot... it was so debilitating, and I felt really hopeless. I suffered on and off throughout my adolescence and early twenties and was only diagnosed with panic disorder in my late twenties. It took that long to realize what was happening to me and for me to access some help. I just wish someone had spotted my symptoms earlier and helped me, because I spent so many years living in terror and feeling so alone.' (Sarah, teacher)

Panic attacks can be triggered by external things (e.g. heights, spiders, frightening or traumatic situations), and also by internal sensations. For example, for those who have panic disorder, the panic attack is often triggered by the sensation of feeling the heart rate increase, or digestive discomfort. Lots of people experience panic attacks, but it can be hard to know what to do when they happen, leaving the young person feeling helpless and out of control. This helplessness can leave them feeling at the mercy of their anxiety and being afraid that a debilitating panic attack could occur at any time in any place. This heightened anxiety inevitably results in a greater incidence of panic attacks. However, there are ways to cope with them and feel better, and this feeling of being in control can effectively help to stop a panic attack in its tracks.

REFLECTION POINT

Take some time to reflect on your understanding of panic attacks. Think about what you may have witnessed, both in yourself and the children and young people you work with. How have you been able to manage these events to date? Do you need to develop your skill set and knowledge base further? Make a list of your questions and discuss these with other staff members on your team. Think about what you currently have in place in your setting to support children and young people when they experience a panic attack. What strategies do staff use? Is there a safe space or base for children and young people to go to when they feel overwhelmed?

The importance of breathing

Understanding how breathing affects our nervous system is vital for informing how we support those having a panic attack. When we breathe in, our blood cells gain oxygen and release carbon dioxide. Quick, shallow breathing can affect this process, contributing to anxiety and panic attacks.

'Learning that I could reduce the panic with breathing techniques was an absolute game-changer! For the first time, I actually felt like I was in control rather than the anxiety always being in control.' (Sarah, teacher)

When people are anxious, they tend to take rapid breaths that come directly from the chest. There is a tendency to hyperventilate by taking fast in-breaths without adequate out-breaths, meaning that the blood is not being properly oxygenated, signalling a stress response that contributes to panic attacks. This is sometimes referred to as chest breathing or thoracic breathing.

On the other hand, diaphragmatic breathing stimulates the parasympathetic branch of the autonomic nervous system, which is part of the nervous system responsible for regulating heartbeat, blood flow, breathing and digestion. This deep breathing can help prevent the fight-or-flight response to a stress-inducing situation or help bring the body out of a panic attack. Newborns automatically breathe this way; it is easy to recognize, as the tummy, rather than the chest, will expand when breathing. This is how most of us breathe while asleep and when in our most relaxed states.

Most people are unaware of how they are breathing. Still, it can be helpful to encourage children to notice so that they can focus their attention on aiming for deep diaphragmatic breathing, rather than shallow chest breathing. You can help children focus on diaphragmatic breathing by lying on the floor with an object (e.g. teddy, book) on their tummy and trying to make it move up and down as they breathe.

REFLECTION POINT

The language we use when talking to anxious children and young people is very important. We need to be very careful not to judge them, to remain calm ourselves, and to reassure them that their feelings will pass and can be managed. Developing a script for yourself when working with an anxious child can be helpful. What language would you use? What are the calming words that would really make a difference to a child in that moment of heightened anxiety? Take some time to think about your language and construct a helpful script that you can make use of and adapt for a range of children and young people.

CASE STUDY

Abrahim was suffering from panic attacks every day and had become reluctant to attend school. He was terrified of being sick at school, and the feeling of nausea that came with the anxiety only made things worse. Abrahim was anxious about feeling sick, and feeling sick because of the anxiety, which created a vicious cycle that felt impossible to break. Abrahim had catastrophic thoughts about being sick in the classroom, and assemblies were his worst nightmare as they felt impossible for him to escape from if he felt unwell.

Aisling, a teaching assistant, recognized Abrahim's symptoms and, together with his parents, they reached an understanding of what was going on for Abrahim. His parents had not realized that the meltdowns that Abrahim had been having were actually panic attacks. Aisling worked with Abrahim to enable him to understand his anxiety, what was happening in his body, and why it made him feel nauseous. He learned what to look out for and some strategies to cope, including challenging his catastrophic thoughts, positive self-talk, mindfulness exercises and breathing techniques. They put together a safety plan (they called it a 'panic plan') for strategies that Abrahim could try when he noticed the panic rising. He identified exercises that worked well for him, including taking a few minutes in a quiet, safe place and doing square breathing for three minutes. He also identified people to whom he could go for help, and a signal that he could use to indicate if he was struggling to self-regulate and needed co-regulation from a trusted adult. Having the tools and the panic plan gave Abrahim a sense of empowerment, which helped him to gain control of his panic attacks.

Questions

1. What symptoms may Aisling have spotted that made her think that Abrahim was experiencing panic attacks?

2. How was the panic plan helpful for Abrahim?

3. Design your own panic plan to use with a student who has panic attacks.

Top tips and strategies

FIRES

Use the FIRES Framework (see Chapter 1) to support children and young people with panic attacks. When dealing with someone who is experiencing a panic attack, pay particular attention to the points shown in Table 8.1.

Table 8.1 FIRES and panic attacks

F	Fast response	If someone is having a panic attack and is in clear distress, it may be that they need support from an adult straight away rather than having any time to prepare for the conversation.
I	Identify needs and risks	If the child is experiencing breathing difficulties, which could be the precursor to a panic attack, encourage them to move to a safe space away from other children or young people, in which they can be supported by an adult who can help them to regulate. If the child is asthmatic and having difficulty breathing, follow your first aid protocol.
R	Reassure	Reassure them that their feelings will pass, that they are safe and that these feelings are normal and common.
E	Empathize and listen	Validate their feelings, even if they do seem irrational to you.
S	Support and signpost	Support them to regulate before sharing with your mental health lead, the designated safeguarding lead and parents/carers where possible. The MHL should use the THRIVE Framework (see Chapter 1) to plan support with the young person and seek support and advice from the local CAMHS.

The role of the supporting adult

The role of the adult is crucial in helping children and young people to co-regulate when in a state of panic. The presence of a calm adult can provide feelings of safety, and modelling strategies such as breathing can help to reduce their anxiety, giving them a sense of control and comfort. This means that the 'Reassure' step of the FIRES Framework takes a leading role during panic attacks.

- *Stay calm* – Use a calm voice, and repetitive phrases (e.g. 'You are safe'). Reassure the pupil that it is just anxiety, and it will all be over soon. Avoid phrases such as 'You are okay' because the child does not feel okay, which may make them feel that you don't understand. It is likely to be more effective if you empathize with their feeling. For example, 'Panic attacks feel really scary, and I know it doesn't feel like it, but you are safe, it will all be over soon, and I will be here to help you until it ends.'

- *Help them to breathe* – Try counting out loud as you both breathe in for five seconds and out for five seconds. Role-modelling this can help them to mirror your calmness and self-regulate.

- *Avoid avoidance* – Those experiencing panic attacks may feel the urge to escape or avoid the situation, but, where possible, encourage them to stay where they are and keep focusing on things in the here and now until they feel calmer. Escaping may provide a quick sense of relief but will only increase future anxiety around the location or situation.

- *Stay with them afterwards* – Take the child or young person to a quiet place to calm down. It can be helpful to get them a drink of cold water. Try to avoid going straight into talking about the panic attack, as the young person may need longer to recover before they are calm enough to problem-solve.

- *Always remember the 3 Rs* – Regulate, Relate and Reason (see Chapter 4).

Support and signpost

When the child or young person is calm, some strategies and techniques can be used to support them in minimizing and managing future panic attacks.

Teach them about panic attacks

Knowledge is power. Panic attacks feel very frightening, but understanding where all of the symptoms are coming from and what is happening in their bodies can be helpful. Also, understanding that breathing deeply can help to reduce the stress response in the body can give the young person some control back.

> 'Knowing that what was happening to me was a panic attack, and knowing what was happening in my body, made it feel a lot less scary.' (Carter, aged 9)

Try to challenge any negative automatic thoughts

In speaking to the young person afterwards, try to identify any negative thoughts that they are having that could be increasing their feelings of panic, (e.g. 'I'm going to die', 'I can't cope', 'I'm going crazy', 'I'll be sick'). Use the CBT strategies described in Chapter 7 to challenge these thoughts gently. For example, ask questions such as:

- 'What is the evidence for that thought?'
- 'What is the evidence against that thought?'
- 'What is a more balanced thought?'
- 'What would I say to a friend who had that thought?'

Teach them to shift their focus when panic starts to rise

Suggest sucking on a mint to help keep them grounded. The mint flavour draws attention to their senses, and the sucking action can be soothing. Alternatively, encourage them to ground their senses through identifying:

- 5 things they can see
- 4 things they can touch or feel
- 3 things they can hear
- 2 things they can smell
- 1 thing they can taste.

Encourage exercise

When they start to feel anxious, encourage them to jump up and down, jog on the spot or do any activity that is physical but not too challenging. The aim is to use up the adrenaline, but raising the heart rate too much can feel like a panic attack, which may increase anxiety. Encourage them to keep focusing on their breathing while doing light physical activity.

Encourage positive self-talk

It can be beneficial to learn phrases to say to themselves during a panic attack. Repeating these phrases can be soothing and can help to engage the parasympathetic branch of the autonomic nervous system, resulting in feelings of calm.

Phrases that you can say to them, or encourage them to say to themselves, include:

- 'I am safe.'
- 'It will pass.'
- 'This is just anxiety.'
- 'Anxiety can't harm me.'
- 'I am in control.'

These can be said aloud or, if they are in a situation where this would not be possible (e.g. exams), in their head.

Breathing techniques

The following breathing techniques can be extremely helpful, and it is strongly advised that you take the time to practise them yourself so that you can effectively model them for the children and young people that you are supporting.

Alternate-nostril breathing

A breathing technique commonly practised in yoga is alternate-nostril breathing. This involves putting your finger over one nostril at a time as you breathe through the other, swapping between nostrils in a regular pattern. This can be tricky at first and result in some giggles, but this can also work in your favour, given that distraction and humour are also excellent ways to relieve anxiety! It is best to practise this type of anxiety-relieving breathing in a seated position, to maintain posture. Encourage children to adopt the FOFBOC position (feet on the floor, bottom on the chair), and to keep their shoulders relaxed.

1. Close your eyes.
2. Block your right nostril with your thumb.
3. Breathe in deeply through your left nostril.
4. Block your left nostril with your ring finger.
5. Open and breathe out through your right nostril.
6. Inhale through your right nostril.

7. Block your right nostril with your thumb.

8. Open and breathe out through your left nostril.

9. Breathe in through your left nostril.

Ask the young person to repeat this until they feel calmer. If they begin to feel lightheaded, encourage them to stop and breathe normally.

Belly breathing

According to research, 20 minutes of deep 'diaphragmatic' breathing every day can reduce anxiety (Hopper et al., 2019). Encourage the young person to get comfortably seated or lie on the floor, and provide them with the following instructions:

1. Place one hand on your upper chest and the other hand on your tummy.

2. Allow your tummy to relax.

3. Inhale slowly through your nose and notice your tummy rising up.

4. Breathe out slowly with your lips slightly pursed as though blowing down a recorder. Your tummy should go down, drawing your tummy button inwards, but also notice the hand on your chest, which should remain still.

Square breathing

Also known as 'box breathing', square breathing is very simple to learn and practise. Ask the child to find something in the room with four sides (e.g. a window, door, a wall, a book, exam paper, etc.), then move their eyes or trace a finger along the sides of the square while completing the following breathing pattern.

1. Start at the bottom left-hand corner and trace up as you breathe in for four seconds.

2. As you trace along the top, hold your breath for four seconds.

3. Exhale for four seconds as you trace down the right-hand side.

4. Hold your breath for four seconds as you trace along the bottom.

5. Keep repeating this pattern until you start to feel more relaxed.

Lion's breath

Lion's breath is a breathing exercise involving sticking your tongue out and roaring like a lion! As with many other breathing exercises, once again, assume the FOFBOC position (feet on floor, bottom on chair).

1. Extend your fingers as far apart as you can.

2. Inhale through your nostrils.

3. Open your mouth wide, extend your tongue, and stretch it downward towards your chin.

4. Exhale vigorously, directing the breath across the base of your tongue.

5. While exhaling, produce a 'ha' sound originating from the depths of your abdomen.

6. Take regular breaths for a brief period.

7. Perform the lion's breath sequence for up to seven repetitions.

REFLECTION POINT

Think about what works for you when using breathing exercises. It's important to remember that any plan needs to be bespoke to the individual. What works for one person may not work for another.

Reference

Hopper, S.I., Murray, S.L., Ferrara, L.R. & Singleton, J.K. (2019) 'Effectiveness of diaphragmatic breathing for reducing physiological and psychological stress in adults: A quantitative systematic review.' *JBI Database of Systematic Reviews and Implementation Reports, 17*(9), 1855–1876. doi:10.11124/JBISRIR-2017-003848

CHAPTER 9

Understanding and Supporting Those with Depression

What is depression?

Depression is the term used to describe low mood, hopelessness and loss of interest, with low mood being the predominant emotion for at least two weeks. Between the ages of eight and puberty, around 2 to 4 percent of children are diagnosed with clinical depression – after puberty, it is around 4 to 8 percent – and it is more commonly diagnosed in girls than boys (Angold & Worthman, 1993). However, this may be because girls are more likely to talk about their feelings and seek support.

The symptoms of depression in children are very similar to those in adults:

- depressed mood most of the day, every day

- apathy and loss of interest or pleasure in activities previously enjoyed

- weight loss when not dieting, or weight gain

- a decrease or increase in appetite

- frequent insomnia, or sleeping too much

- extreme restlessness or lethargy

- fatigue or loss of energy

- feelings of worthlessness or inappropriate guilt

- diminished ability to think or concentrate

- recurrent thoughts of death and suicidal thoughts.

Children may be more likely to seem irritable than sad, and more likely to have insomnia than sleep too much. You may notice that the child does not want to do the things they usually enjoy, avoids people, complains they cannot sleep well, and has a change in their eating patterns. They might start being critical about themselves or say they feel useless. They may not do as well as usual at school, because they cannot concentrate or lack the energy and motivation to finish work.

Some of the symptoms of depression – particularly restlessness and finding it difficult to concentrate – overlap with attention deficit hyperactivity disorder (ADHD), so it can make it more difficult to recognize depression in a child with ADHD.

School staff should consider a referral to CAMHS, or encourage parents to seek advice from a GP about the possibility of depression, if they notice that:

- the child has stopped doing the things they usually enjoy

- their personality has changed

- they avoid friends and communicate less with staff/parents/ significant caregivers

- they seem more unhappy than usual.

'I didn't really know that there was anything wrong with me. It crept up on me slowly and I just felt sad all of the time, but I was so used to feeling sad that I didn't really question it at the time. I just thought that was how life would be for me.' (Lois, aged 17)

Treating depression

Depression can be managed with several treatments, such as CBT and SSRIs.

Cognitive behavioural therapy (CBT) helps people identify unhelpful thoughts about themselves, others and the world around them. CBT encourages them to challenge these thoughts. (See Chapter 7 for more information.)

SSRIs are a type of antidepressant medication. SSRI stands for 'selective serotonin reuptake inhibitor'. Usually antidepressants have a delay of at least two weeks before they start to work, and this delay can often be up to six weeks. This early stage of treatment is when any side effects are at their greatest, so it is likely that the child or young person will need the highest level of support during this time. There are lots of different types of antidepressants and, with appropriate medical advice, it may be worth trying an alternative medication if the first type of antidepressant doesn't suit a particular child. Antidepressants are usually taken for at least six months and the child's doctor will advise when they are ready to gradually come off medication.

In general, approximately 10 percent of children and young people with depression recover without treatment within three months. However, on average, without treatment, 50 percent remain depressed after one year, and 20–30 percent continue suffering after two years (National Collaborating Centre for Mental Health, 2005).

REFLECTION POINT

Take some time to think about your knowledge and understanding of depression. It is important to be aware of your own experiences of low mood, and to analyse what did and did not help you to get through such times in your life. Recognizing that we all experience low mood at some point is essential. It is also important to remember that, when we are supporting children and young people who are depressed, this may be triggering for us as individuals as well. It is vital to access the relevant support mechanisms in your own context.

Jot down some of the things that did or did not help you when you felt low. Also, make a list of all the different support systems that you currently have in your life, and think about which work the best for you and why.

Top tips and strategies
When to act and what to do

Talking to the young person about how they feel is a big step in the right direction. However, it is important to remember that an open conversation may not always be possible, given the tendency for those with depression to withdraw. It is, therefore, essential that you continue to monitor the child or young person in terms of their functioning, but also share your concerns with the DSL, the school's mental health lead or educational psychologist; if you are worried about any risk of suicide or self-harm, it is vital to seek professional advice and support in a timely way.

Very often, as the nurturing adult, it can be tempting to rush into finding a solution. However, it is always best to engage in a dialogue with the young person, to find a way forward together. Coping with depression is never a quick fix and always takes time. Discussing various options, including specialist helplines offering confidential support, and a listening ear can be helpful at this stage in the process. Which is why it is very important to keep detailed notes of any interactions that you have with the child or young person in your attempts to support them through this period of low mood. This will inform any further support that the child or young person may be allocated if they are subsequently referred to specialist support, either via the MHL or their general practitioner.

'I just wanted friends and family to treat me normally.' (Ben, aged 16)

Keeping to routines, both in the school and the family context, can be very helpful for the child with low mood. Maintaining ordinary, every-day activities, alongside planning small events to look forward to and enjoy together, can also be beneficial. This is because it provides positive distractions for the child or young person.

Talking to the child/young person

When we are working with children with low mood it can be very difficult to engage with them initially. However, making time to talk is the most important first step we can all take. The key to this is to think ahead and prepare thoroughly, to ensure that those initial conversations go as well as they can. Always remember to speak to the MHL and/or DSL before having the conversation with the young person, to be certain that you have the full picture, and ease them gently into the discussion.

Here are some ideas that may help you with those first conversations:

- *Start slowly* – Initiate a conversation with the young person about something safe and familiar to begin with, so that they feel safe and at ease when speaking to you.

- *Use 'I' statements* – Talk to the child on their level and explain that you are worried about how they might be feeling and that you want to help them. Phrases that use 'I' rather than 'you' can feel less confrontational. For example, 'I've noticed that you seem a bit down – how are you?' is less judgemental and is more inviting than 'You seem down'.

- *Don't force them to talk* – The young person may not feel comfortable or ready to talk, and that is okay. Just reassure them that you are there if they want to talk, and continue to regularly check in with them, to provide opportunities for them to talk, safe in the knowledge that you are there for them and really care. Always share your concerns with the MHL and/or DSL.

- *Ask 'open questions'* – Ask questions that allow the child to say how they are feeling rather than give you a yes/no answer. A good opener is 'How are you feeling?' or 'What's on your mind?', then see where the conversation goes from there.

- *Contain your own anxiety* – It is very normal to feel anxious about a young person who seems to be struggling with their mental health. To open up, young people need to feel that you can handle their difficult thoughts and emotions. Although it is crucial to look after yourself throughout this, when talking try to focus on their feelings and what you can do to help.

- *Take your time* – Make sure that you initiate the conversation in a timely manner (think F – Fast response), but at a time when you can fully give them your time and attention. It may well take a number of conversations for them to open up, and that's okay. Take your time and be there for the child, at the right pace for them. Remember that there is no quick fix, but make sure to keep talking on a regular basis.

Referring for further help

You may well play a key role in the recovery plan from depression for the child or young person that you work with. However, in addition to working closely with their parents/carers, it may also be necessary to make a referral to the general practitioner (GP) or Child and Adolescent Mental Health Service (CAMHS), who may prescribe specific therapies or treatments. Remember that therapies and treatments vary depending on individual circumstances, and it is important that the child finds the right fit for them.

Watchful monitoring

If the depression is mild, in the first instance, the GP may recommend 'watchful monitoring', also sometimes referred to as 'watchful waiting'. This is where the young person's wellbeing is closely monitored for signs and symptoms of depression, to assess its severity and the impact of simple lifestyle changes (e.g. exercise). A two-week follow-up appointment will usually be arranged to see how things have progressed.

Therapeutic intervention

If there is no improvement during the 'watchful monitoring' phase, or if the GP assesses the depression as being moderate or severe, they may make a referral to a therapist for 'talking therapy'. This may include treatments such as CBT, interpersonal therapy and family therapy, all of which are recommended by NICE as having a good evidence base for effectiveness for depression (NICE, 2019). CBT is one of the most effective and frequently used treatments to reduce depressive symptoms.

Medication

Initially, a GP will not usually suggest medication if the depression is mild. However, this will be reviewed, and medication may be prescribed at a later point if symptoms worsen. Psychological help is often enough on its own to treat depression, but sometimes medication will also be prescribed if the depression is severe.

> 'I was worried that the doctor would make me take antidepressants and I didn't really want to do that. It was a relief when they just sent me to talk to someone.' (Sam, aged 14)

> 'The tablets they gave me made me feel weird and sick, and I really hated taking them at first, but after a few weeks, the side effects went, and I felt so much better. I don't know where I would have ended up without them – they saved my life.' (Trina, aged 16)

Getting help

- Children under 16 should be referred to the local Child and Adolescent Mental Health Service (CAMHS). Through this service, they may receive support from a psychologist, counsellor, therapist or other practitioners trained in wellbeing support (e.g. education mental health practitioner).

- Some parents may choose to find their own therapist, who should be registered with and accredited by a professional body such as the British Association for Behavioural and Cognitive Therapies (BABCP).

- Local charities also sometimes offer counselling. Again, these professionals should be registered and accredited by a professional body, such as the Health Care Professions Council (HCPC), United Kingdom Council for Psychotherapy (UKCP) or British Association for Counselling and Psychotherapy (BACP) and should be experienced in working with children and young people.

FIRES

As with the other topics covered in this toolkit, the FIRES acronym can guide you in responding in a safe, supportive way (see Table 9.1):

Table 9.1 FIRES and depression

F	Fast response	Proactively approach the child or young person about your concerns.
I	Identify needs and risks	Look for signs of self-harm, hopelessness or suicidal thoughts, and don't be afraid to ask those sensitive questions.
R	Reassure	Reassure them that, with help, they can begin to feel better. Instil a sense of hope and optimism.
E	Empathize and listen	Listen, if and when they are ready to talk to you, showing genuine care and patience.
S	Support and signpost	Share your observations and meeting notes with the school's mental health lead, the designated safeguarding lead and parents or carers where possible, as appropriate. MHL should use the THRIVE Framework (see Chapter 1) to plan support with the young person. If needed, refer to CAMHS and encourage self-help, signposting the child or young person to sources of support, both in school and online.

CASE STUDY

Julie, a teaching assistant, had noticed that Seth hadn't seemed himself lately. He was withdrawn, was always on his own with his headphones in, not engaging with anyone. She wasn't sure if his behaviour was just a 'moody teenage phase', and every time she casually asked him how he was, he just said that he was tired. Julie knew that changes in behaviour, withdrawal and persistent tiredness or difficulty sleeping could also signal depression. She spoke first with the MHL and DSL and found out that a concern had also been raised by one of his teachers, as he had seemed irritable, and his grades had dipped. It was agreed that Julie would speak to Seth.

While he initially said he was 'fine', after weeks of building a rapport, Seth admitted that he had lost interest in a lot of things that he used to enjoy, and he described himself as feeling 'numb'. Seth told Julie that he was feeling down but had not had any suicidal thoughts. Seth wasn't sure about going to the GP as he didn't want to make a 'big deal' out of it, but reluctantly agreed to speak to his parents about how he was feeling and make an appointment. The doctor did a questionnaire with Seth to look at whether he met the criteria for a diagnosis of depression, and to what degree of severity. The GP decided that 'watchful monitoring' for two weeks would be helpful and encouraged Seth to try to re-engage with activities that he had previously enjoyed, and to try adding some regular exercise into his routine.

Julie was involved in this process of monitoring, through supporting Seth to complete a reflective log of how he was feeling and the impact that different things had on his mood. Building this rapport, and having consistent support from a trusted adult, really helped Seth to feel safe enough to talk, knowing that he would be listened to fully. After two weeks of watchful monitoring, the GP suggested two more weeks of the same, and through the relationship with Julie, as well as the self-help strategies that he had adopted, Seth no longer met the criteria for depression by the four-week check.

Questions

1. What signs of depression was Seth presenting with?

2. If you were asked to support a young person with depression

who was being monitored, rather than given treatment, how would you feel?

3. What could you do to support a young person with depression in school?

Support and signpost

As the adult taking on the role of a nurturer, it is important to encourage the child or young person to identify, access, then make use of a range of self-help ideas and strategies, which can help to reduce their levels of anxiety and increase their capacity to manage stress on a daily basis. You can help by:

- encouraging the child or young person to talk about their feelings to friends and key family members who can help them

- referring them to appropriate self-help books, apps and websites

- encouraging them to take daily exercise and have a healthy diet, avoiding alcohol if possible; constructing an exercise and relaxation diary may be helpful to support them in recording and monitoring their activities

- teaching and modelling a range of relaxation strategies; this is essential and should include visualization, mindfulness-based stress-reduction activities and specific grounding tools and strategies

- encouraging them to practise gratitude and kindness on a daily basis; this might involve keeping a positive journal in which they record every day three kind acts, three things that they are grateful for and any positive events

- ensuring that they get enough sleep and have a healthy sleep routine

- encouraging them to get out in nature, to be physical and active, topping up on their endorphins and vitamin D

- encouraging fun activities with friends or family members, which can distract them from their low mood.

'Focusing on three positives about each day was really hard at first

but, after a few weeks, I started to just notice good things without really having to try so much.' (Saffia, aged 17)

Developing a wellbeing plan

All of us can benefit from making a wellbeing plan which includes a range of tools and strategies designed to maintain a positive mood and combat or reduce periods of low mood or depression. Alongside the self-help ideas listed above, it can be helpful to specifically focus on developing an awareness and ability to make use of key tools from cognitive behavioural therapy (CBT).

The following five strategies were inspired by CBT to relieve stress and increase mood:

- Drop the plastic plates!

- Take a break.

- Challenge your own thoughts.

- Mood monitoring.

- Take control.

Trying these strategies, described in more detail below, yourself can help you to feel better informed on which strategies might be effective for pupils that you work with.

Drop the plastic plates!

When your to-do list starts to stack up, your stress levels increase to meet the rising demands. Take time to prioritize these tasks, rather than feeling overwhelmed by thinking that everything needs to be done NOW. People often describe themselves as 'spinning plates' when they have too many demands and feel the struggle to juggle them all. Imagine that some of your demands are your finest china plates, and some are plastic picnic plates. Think about which are the plastic plates that you can drop and pick up later without any damage being done.

To start, list what you need to do that day, and rate how important each task is. Some tasks are likely to be absolutely vital (the finest china plates), and some comparatively unimportant (the plastic plates!). Acknowledge that the tasks at the bottom of the list are not only improbable to be accomplished within the day but might also be unnecessary.

Remove those items from the list and concentrate your efforts on the most crucial priorities.

Take a break

During a busy school day, making time for yourself can be difficult, but recharging those batteries is vital. Use your breaks wisely – take the opportunity to go for a mindful walk, have a hot comforting drink, talk to a colleague, do a breathing exercise, or have some time alone – do whatever makes you feel refreshed and ready to face the challenges that may arise. Try to avoid staying in the classroom or eating at your desk!

Challenge your own thoughts

Most of us have been guilty at some point of 'catastrophizing' – thinking in which we imagine that the worst possible outcome is the most likely. In addition to making us feel stressed, this type of black-and-white thinking can lead to a sense of impending doom that is probably not justified or realistic.

Try asking yourself some thought-challenging questions, such as 'Has this ever happened before?' or 'What's the likelihood of something terrible happening?' In most cases, the probability will be very low. If this feels difficult, and the catastrophe still feels very probable, try experimenting by comparing your probability estimate with someone else's, or ask yourself what you think someone else might say. This can sometimes be the reality check we need to help ourselves move to a more realistic thought.

Mood monitoring

This CBT activity can be an effective way to recognize and challenge negative thoughts. Find a pen and paper and give yourself five minutes. In that time, draw three columns on the paper. In the first, write down the stressful event (e.g. 'Monday at 2 p.m.: Meeting with line manager'). In the second, write down the feelings that you are experiencing (e.g. disorganized, anxious) and rate them between 1 and 10, with 10 being 'completely overwhelmed'. In the third column, spend the rest of the five minutes writing all the thoughts that you are having about the event.

Put the paper into an envelope and don't look at it until the next day. Once you've taken yourself out of that emotional headspace and distanced yourself from the situation, look back at what you wrote down.

The aim is that you can now look at the thoughts and feelings from a more objective, rational standpoint, which will make the thoughts easier to challenge. Doing this over time will help you notice the thinking traps (catastrophizing, mind-reading, fortune-telling, black-and-white thinking, etc.) that you fall into most, so you can avoid these in future.

Take control

When you feel out of control in a situation, reduce your stress by reminding yourself of what you can control. Ask yourself what you can do to improve a situation – even if you feel powerless, you can always control your reactions. Focusing on what's within your control will help to remind you that you can impact your own outcomes.

REFLECTION POINT

How would you use these tools when supporting a child or young person? How would you adapt them?

References

Angold, A. & Worthman C.W. (1993) 'Puberty onset of gender differences in rates of depression: A developmental, epidemiologic and neuroendocrine perspective.' *Journal of Affective Disorders, 29,*145–158.

National Collaborating Centre for Mental Health (2005) *Depression in Children and Young People: Identification and Management in Primary, Community and Secondary Care.* Leicester: British Psychological Society.

National Institute for Health and Care Excellence (NICE) (2019) *Depression in Children and Young People: Identification and Management.* London: National Institute for Health and Clinical Excellence.

CHAPTER 10

Grief, Loss and Bereavement

Grief is our response to the loss of someone or something to which we feel an emotional bond. Grief tends to be thought of as an emotional response, but it can also impact us physically, cognitively and spiritually. Grief is often associated with loss through bereavement, but it can also be felt in response to parental abandonment, divorce, a pet dying, the loss of a possession (e.g. your home) or a friend moving away. Grief is often characterized by feelings of prolonged sadness and emotional pain, meaning that the presentation can look similar to that described in the chapter on depression. However, in most cases, grief is not akin to a mental health disorder. It is a normal and natural reaction to loss.

The diagnosis of grief

Before the publication of the fifth edition of the *Diagnostic and Statistical Manual of Mental Disorders* (DSM-5: APA, 2013), a bereavement exclusion existed, whereby a person could not receive a diagnosis of 'major depressive disorder' if they had experienced the death of a loved one within the past two months. The DSM-5 now states a person can still experience major depression while also experiencing bereavement. However, there is a clear distinction between the low mood brought about by loss and that of a mental health condition. Whereas grief often causes a fluctuation of pain and sadness, followed by moments of happiness reflecting on memories from the past, a person experiencing symptoms of major depressive disorder will feel almost constant negativity.

Another distinguishing factor between grief and major depression is the person's opinion of themselves. Associated with major depression are feelings of self-loathing and worthlessness, whereas grief and bereavement do not usually impact on a person's self-esteem. Through these distinctions, it should be possible to determine when a person might be feeling grief as the result of a recent loss, and when they are experiencing a depressive episode and might require additional support from outside agencies.

The DSM-5 also contains the diagnosis of 'persistent complex bereavement disorder' (PCBD). To obtain a diagnosis of PCBD, the grief experienced must be so debilitating that the person is no longer able to engage in everyday life. In the case of children, they must have displayed these difficulties for more than six months following a bereavement. Adults must display these difficulties for more than 12 months following a bereavement. PCBD often co-exists with other disorders (such as anxiety disorders or depression), and people with a lower quality of life, poorer academic achievement and impaired social functioning are more likely to experience PCBD.

In the context of the recent COVID-19 pandemic, it is highly likely that we will see more adults and children displaying PCBD, given the heightened stress levels and traumatic losses many may have experienced during this time. These experiences may have also had a detrimental impact on those with pre-existing mental health issues or specific special or complex needs.

The grieving process
So, what do we know about grief?

Grief is a normal, essential response to the death of a loved one. When someone that we care about dies, it is normal and natural to feel a range of different emotions. People grieve for different lengths of time. It can be short-lived or last a long time, depending on the personality involved, the closeness of the relationship, the circumstances of the death and previous losses suffered.

This grief can often take the form of several clearly defined stages (Kübler-Ross, 1969). This is not necessarily a linear process, and it is now accepted that people move backwards and forwards between these stages as they grieve.

1. Denial

2. Anger

3. Bargaining

4. Depression

5. Acceptance

Denial

The first reaction to a death is often shock, disbelief and denial. This is likely to happen whenever our model of the world is upset. The person may feel numb, going through the day automatically. They may go very quiet and not want to speak to anyone, or they may have times when they feel anxious and in a panic. The person can behave as if nothing has happened, or as if the dead person were still around. For example, they might lay a place at the table for them or go to ring them up and invite them out. They might dream that the dead person is still alive and has not really died. This stage usually occurs in the first fortnight after a death. It may last for only a few minutes or for weeks.

Anger

During this stage, the person gradually realizes what it means to them to have lost someone they care about. This growing awareness can sometimes trigger a number of emotions, including anger. The person may feel angry and want to blame someone; for example, a doctor or someone else involved if there was an accident. Sometimes, the person may be furious with whoever has died because they have left them.

Bargaining

It can be very difficult to accept that something so painful and final can happen and that there is nothing that we can do to change it. Sometimes, the grieving person may feel guilty, even if there is no good reason. For example, they may feel terrible because the last time they talked to the person who has died they had an argument. If there has been an accident, they may feel that this was somehow their fault and go through a string of 'if only' thoughts – for example, 'If only I had been there...' or 'If only I hadn't shouted ...'.

Depression

During this stage, the bereaved person begins to feel the despair, the emptiness, the pain of the loss. The grieving person may feel sad and depressed. They may feel as if nothing matters or may become anxious. They may feel physical pain or very empty inside. They may cry often, even when there is no obvious reason for them to be reminded of the person who has died.

Sometimes, the grieving person may not know quite what they are feeling but develop symptoms or behave in unusual ways. For example, they may be more likely to become ill, find it difficult to get to sleep and start biting their nails. They may either eat far more than usual or lose interest in eating. They may not want to go to school and, if they do, they may find it difficult to concentrate. They may find it hard to finish their homework or to remember what they are supposed to be doing. They may not be able to think clearly.

Acceptance

This generally occurs in the second year after the death has been relived, at the first anniversary. The bereaved person is able to adjust to life without the deceased and begins to invest energy elsewhere. Eventually, the grieving person will be able to get on with life as before. They will, of course, continue to remember the person who has died, but this will not affect them in the same way.

Reactions of children and young people

The reactions of children and young people depend first of all on their understanding of what death means, and this understanding develops as they get older. Table 10.1 briefly summarizes this growing understanding at each key stage of their development.

Table 10.1 Children and young people's growing understanding of death

Age	Understanding
Up to 3 years	No understanding of death (rather a separation) Can explore being and nonbeing through games Can sense adult feelings and require nonverbal communication for reassurance

cont.

Age	Understanding
3 to 6 years	Aware that death is different or 'special' Unaware of the inevitability, universality and irreversibility of death 'Magical thinking' can lead to self-blame
6 to 10 years	Beginning to understand that death is final Sense of morality means they may associate death with retribution for wrong-doing May appear outwardly unaffected due to denial
10 to 12 years	Understand that death is final and irreversible Focus on both biological and emotional aspects of death Also, aware that they too can die – death is personal, universal and real
Adolescence	Adult-like understanding of death May inappropriately assume the roles of the dead person

REFLECTION POINT

Try to think back to your own childhood and what your own understanding of death was at that time – possibly in your early years and teenage years. Think about how this understanding may have changed and the impact of any encounters with grief and loss that you witnessed or personally experienced.

In children, the stages of grief may manifest themselves in the following reactions:

- Children, like adults, will enter a period of shock, which can last for a few hours or up to a week. It can manifest itself by the child going through daily life mechanically, automatically smiling on cue, or being apprehensive. They may have periods of panic. Alternatively, they may become withdrawn and gaze into space for long periods.

- The death of a close relative heightens our sense of vulnerability and, for children, death and separation are synonymous. They may:

  - become very anxious about being separated from parents for any reason

- be reluctant to go to school
- lose concentration when at school
- seem depressed
- be more prone to infection (e.g. colds, ear infections and tummy upsets)
- bite nails or cuticles, pick at their skin, twiddle with their hair
- develop a fear of the dark (which may last for years)
- have difficulty going to sleep
- have nightmares
- develop a phobia about hospitals, nurses and doctors.

- Regression to an earlier stage of development is common.

- Food can become important. Some children will eat and eat, to fill up the emptiness they feel inside. They may hoard food and secrete it away. Others, though, will lose interest in eating. This phase usually only lasts a comparatively short time.

- Sadness and anger need to be expressed, but children are often afraid and confused about venting their feelings, as they do not know what is allowed.

- Some children may be frightened to ask questions and will only talk to 'outsiders'. Other children only want to talk about the tragedy to the immediate family.

The Kübler-Ross Grief Cycle, described above, is often criticized for suggesting that grief is a process that is worked through in a logical fashion, without relapse. In contrast, Stroebe and Schut (1999) put forward the idea of a 'Dual Process Model of Coping with Bereavement', whereby the person who is experiencing grief fluctuates between engaging in loss-oriented actions and restoration-oriented actions. During periods of bereavement, we can become fixated on the loss, expressing feelings of depression, denial, loss of a connection, or struggling to complete other tasks because the grief is so strong. However, we can then switch to restoration-oriented processes, where we are able to accept the loss we have experienced and begin to adjust to the reality that has resulted from the loss.

When observing grief expressed by children, this is often referred to as 'puddle jumping', where a child can present as extremely emotional and vulnerable one minute, and then happily engage in an unrelated activity the next. This can be challenging for teachers, as the child's mood swings are often hard to predict. For family members who are also experiencing grief, this can be very difficult, as the child can appear almost flippant in their understanding of their loss while engaging in restoration-oriented activities.

> 'I prepared myself to tell her about grandma dying, thinking she'd be inconsolable, but she just gave me a hug and asked if she could go back outside to play!' (Michelle, parent)

Tonkin (1996) presents an alternative approach to understanding grief, which is often considered more child-friendly than the previous theories mentioned. Within this theory, it is proposed that the 'size' or intensity of grief that you experience when someone dies remains constant throughout your life. However, as time passes and you begin to experience new things, your life becomes more enriched and grows and develops around your grief. Although your grief remains the same, your life experiences become greater and so your grief feels somewhat smaller in comparison. This theory offers the child or young person reassurance that the person who has died will never be forgotten, while also providing hope that the pain the child is experiencing as a result of grief will not persist at the same intensity for ever.

What does seem to be the case is that, for most people, the grieving process can take approximately two years, but this is clearly influenced by individual circumstances and contexts and is person-specific.

> 'I'm not sure I'll ever be over it. Everyone else seemed to move on after the funeral and went back to normal, but I still miss her so much and think about her all the time. When does it get easier?' (Sara, aged 18, speaking about the loss of her friend six months previously)

Expressing grief

We now know that many people do not pass through the stages of grief smoothly. This process may be made more difficult for children by the natural reaction of adults who seek to protect them from further distress, so avoid talking about the deceased or enabling the child to attend the funeral. Children and young people may also be surrounded by a grieving family and feel that they should not add to any distress by showing their own emotions.

Without the opportunities to express their grief, alongside a clear understanding that grief is not always sequential but often cyclical, some children and young people may get stuck and find it difficult to move forward in living with their loss. This may involve them attempting to replace their loved one by substituting another significant adult in their life, but it may also include displays of aggression, discipline problems, antisocial behaviour or emotionally based school avoidance. It is, therefore, vital to remain vigilant in monitoring children and young people who have lost a loved one to ensure that if they do present as stuck in their grief, they are provided with the appropriate level of therapeutic support from a specialist bereavement counsellor.

CASE STUDY

Tilly was six years old when her mum died. Her mum had been diagnosed with terminal cancer a year earlier, meaning that Tilly had seen her mum being very unwell and in a lot of pain. She had some understanding that her mum was going to die, but not knowing when it would happen had been very traumatic for Tilly. She had been scared every morning that Mum would not wake up, and worried every day that her mum would not still be alive when she finished school.

Marion, a teaching assistant, had been liaising closely with Tilly's parents in the months beforehand, to understand how she was coping at home and what support she may need over time. Marion had been able to build a rapport with Tilly by meeting with her once a week to talk and play games in the lead-up to her mother's death, so that she would be well placed to provide emotional support as a trusted adult both before and after the bereavement. Marion was anxious about how to support Tilly and felt powerless, as she wanted to make it better for her. Marion realized that taking the pain away wasn't possible, or even what Tilly needed at that time, and instead she provided her with an empathetic listening ear, a shoulder to cry on and a consistent, safe person with whom to share her feelings.

In the first few weeks, Marion told Tilly that she could come and find her any time that she was struggling. However, to Marion's surprise, Tilly stayed in class and seemed mostly to be coping well. Tilly's dad explained that she was very upset at home, but that school was a welcome distraction for her, where she could feel almost normal for a few hours. After the funeral, Marion asked Tilly whether she would like to do some activities together to remember her mum. By this point, three weeks had passed, the initial shock had subsided and the outpourings of love and sympathy that had helped Tilly through those first few weeks had started to reduce. Everyone else was moving on, and Tilly was only now really starting to realize that her mum had gone for ever.

She agreed to do some activities with Marion. They made a memory box, and Tilly drew pictures of herself with her mum as she talked about the things that she loved most about her. Marion continued to be a consistent, trusted adult for Tilly to talk to over the course of the year. At times, Tilly wanted to talk; at times, she just wanted to play games with Marion; and at other times, she asked Marion blunt questions about her mum's death, which in other circumstances might have seemed a bit morbid and inappropriate! Marion recognized that this was Tilly trying to understand death and process what had happened to her mum. They were also likely to be questions that she knew she couldn't ask at home, where all of her family were equally devastated.

One of the things that Tilly had said she was most upset about was that she had no one to do her hair nicely for school, as Dad wasn't very good at plaits. They agreed that Tilly could come and check in with Marion each morning at the start of school and, as Marion plaited her hair, Tilly would speak to Marion about how she was feeling. This really helped Tilly to cope during that difficult time.

Questions

1. What do you think is the most important way for a member of school staff to offer support following a bereavement?

2. What learning points will you carry with you from Marion's experience of supporting Tilly?

Top tips and strategies

It is important, first of all, not to underestimate the ways in which the grief of others can retrigger our own memories and experience of loss. Before you begin to work with the child or young person who is experiencing a loss of this nature, it is essential that you understand how you may have worked through your own grief and learned to live with the ongoing pain of loss. It is also vital that, if you are currently experiencing the significant loss of a loved one, you are very careful about attempting to support others in a similar situation. This is something you may wish to discuss with your line manager prior to taking on work of this nature.

Key strategies for supporting children with grief and loss

The most effective strategy for supporting a child or young person who is experiencing a bereavement is to be available for them so they can talk about what is happening. It might be that they wish to talk about their feelings in the 'here and now', or they might want to discuss concerns they have about the past or future. Alternatively, they might want to share memories of the person who has died but feel they cannot speak with other family members, as it might cause upset. The key things to remember when supporting a child or young person to talk about grief and loss are:

- *Tell the truth* – It is important to encourage parents to be open and honest with their child so that they can gain as clear an understanding of the situation as possible. The 'Goldilocks principle' can be useful here – not too much information, but not too little as this may lead children to conjure up worse scenarios in their minds and become confused. This is not always easy, particularly in more challenging situations, such as a murder, accidental overdose or suicide. Keep in close communication with the parents so that you understand what the child knows, what they want them to know, and other wishes that might be important to be mindful of in supporting the child (e.g. the religious beliefs of the family).

- *Avoid using metaphors* – Use words such as 'died' and 'dead' rather than 'gone to a better place', 'gone to sleep' or 'is no longer with us'. This can be very confusing for a child, and they might believe that, ultimately, that person will come back at some point. This is particularly true for younger children, who have not yet established that death is a permanent and irreversible state.

- *Avoid telling the child not to worry or be sad* – Adults naturally wish to reassure children and remove any pain or suffering. However, it is important to recognize that there is a range of intense emotions that are associated with the grieving process and that these all serve to support the child or young person through the experience. It is normal to feel sad, scared, angry or guilty following a loss, and you should support the child by acknowledging and normalizing these emotions, rather than attempting to dismiss them.

- *It's okay to cry* – Crying is something which has an amount of social stigma attached to it. This is particularly the case for older students and male students. As with acknowledging and normalizing the emotions being displayed by the child or young person, you should also acknowledge and normalize crying. To this extent, it is okay for *you* to cry too. Providing support for the child does not mean that you have to be 'strong' and show no emotion. Grief is something which affects everybody and can generate strong emotional reactions in people. It is perfectly fine for you to express these emotions alongside the child. However, it is also important that you are aware of the impact that this is having on you and, if you feel that you are not the best person to support a child due to your own personal circumstances, you should acknowledge this to yourself and discuss with your line manager.

- *Provide reassurance* – As the child begins to gain an understanding of what has happened, they are likely to feel unsure or unsafe. For example, 'If this has happened to Mummy, what's to stop it happening to Daddy?' They will, therefore, require lots of reassurance. This should let the child know that their reaction to the situation is normal (as mentioned above). They should also be reassured that they did not cause the incident and that other people in their lives are safe. This is particularly true for children who are at the 'magical thinking' stage of development.

Depending on the relationship that the child or young person had with the person who has died, they might require additional support in processing feelings such as guilt – for example, if they had previously experienced conflict with that person.

- *Prepare for a variety of emotions* – Children can react in many different ways to death. Depending on their understanding of death, they may appear unaffected. Alternatively, they might 'puddle jump', in which case it is really important that, when you prepare to talk about death with a child, you are also prepared for a variety of emotions to come from them, and that you are able to interpret these emotions as the child coping with processing the information they are receiving, rather than a callous or unemotional response to an upsetting situation.

- *Repeat as necessary* –It might take a number of discussions before the child is able to process and understand what is being said. An element of this might be shock, when, for example, someone has died unexpectedly. However, this can also be related to the child's age and stage of development in regard to understanding death, and so you might find you are having the same conversation with them on a number of occasions as they attempt to make sense of what is going on around them.

Some other top tips to guide your conversations:

- Encourage them to ask questions. Tell them not to be afraid of making themselves sadder by asking these questions and talking about the death of their loved one.

- Help them to recognize that it is okay to feel happy as well as sad. Just because they might be having a good day and enjoying something, it does not mean that they have forgotten their loved one.

- Use appropriate story books or literature to prompt the conversations. Also, make use of appropriate resources to support such conversations.

- Keep to normal routines as much as possible and encourage them to attend the usual after-school clubs or activities, as appropriate.

- Check out any relevant support groups that may be available to the child or young person, both in and outside of the school context, and discuss whether or not these may be helpful to them.

- Ensure that the child has access to a relevant helpline so that they can discuss their thoughts and feelings with a professional as and when they need to.

- Encourage the child or young person to keep a journal to help process their feelings further.

- Ensure that fun times are actually scheduled into the child or young person's day.

- Ensure that the child or young person feels kept in mind and loved by those who are still there to nurture them.

The importance of remembering

To look forward to the future, we need to be able to look back, process what has happened and hold on to our memories. Grief is not about forgetting the person who has died but finding ways to remember them. When a person that we love dies, our feelings remain, and we need to find an outlet to express those feelings. Commonly, those who have been bereaved fear the further loss of their memories of their loved one. These memories are particularly precious because they are all that remain, and no new memories can be made. Supporting them through developing ways to remember can provide great comfort, these may include:

- *Memory box* – Create a special box to keep precious possessions such as photographs, dried flowers from the funeral, a piece of their jewellery or other items that had importance to them.

- *Visiting the grave* – For some, visiting the grave of their loved one is a fundamental part of their grieving process. It sustains a connection with the person, setting aside the rest of the world to communicate with them. This may involve sharing news, showing sadness and expressing love through gestures like flowers.

- *Memory book* – Making a book of photographs, poems, drawings, thoughts and letters can support a young person in expressing and processing their grief and providing them with a way to remember in the future.

- *Planting trees or shrubs* – When someone has died within the school community (e.g. a staff member or child), young people may like to establish a lasting memorial by planting a tree or shrub, often with a commemorative plaque. Ensuring the selection of a hardy tree is vital to minimize the risk of it dying and compounding the sense of loss already experienced. Equally important is planting it in a location accessible to the family so they can visit when they wish.

- *Candles* – Lighting a special candle and reading a prayer or poem can be a simple but poignant way of marking an anniversary, birthday or any other significant date.

- *Writing a diary* – Keeping a diary chronicling the journey through grief can be helpful for those mourning the death of a loved one, for several reasons. Expressing emotions in writing can provide a cathartic release for some, alleviating some of the pain. The diary also serves as a reference point, allowing individuals to revisit their past emotions and recognize their growth and resilience despite the challenges.

When a death impacts on many children and young people in the community

Unfortunately, there are times when, rather than supporting one child or young person with a loss or bereavement, you may find yourself needing to support many children at once. This is particularly likely when a child at school has died or following the death of a member of staff. Such occasions are often called 'critical incidents' as these are beyond the scope of what a school could be expected to cope with alone. These incidents tend to trigger a response from the local authority, meaning that support will be deployed from the local authority (e.g. educational psychologists) and local charities to support staff, children and families in your school community. In these cases, the following guidance can be shared with school staff.

✳ **SUPPORTING CHILDREN AND YOUNG PEOPLE FOLLOWING A BEREAVEMENT: GUIDANCE FOR SCHOOL STAFF**

Following difficult events, school staff are often in the best position to support children and young people with their emotions. Some will seek support and guidance from each other, or from their parents, but it is also likely that some children will want to discuss what has happened with you. Please use this guidance to support any discussions that you have.

1. Although it may feel very difficult, allow pupils to express their feelings to you as you will be one of their main sources of comfort and safety. It will also help you to identify if any pupils are really struggling to cope now, and in the weeks and months to come.

2. Don't worry about knowing what to say. The most important thing is to listen and empathize. Everyone feels helpless in situations like this, and no one is looking to you to make it better.

3. Don't be afraid to express some emotion in a calm and measured way. Children will take their cues from you and assess what is normal based on your reactions.

4. Reassure the children that people react in lots of different ways when difficult events occur, and that all of the emotions that they are feeling are a *normal reaction to an abnormal situation*.

5. Focus on identifying coping strategies that they have used previously, and support networks that they can use over the coming weeks. This will help them to regain a sense of control.

6. Although it is good to provide children with a safe place to express their emotions, it is also important to resume normality as soon as possible, as this will provide children with feelings of security and safety. Continue with lessons as normal, although it may be advisable to avoid challenging new content.

7. There are a team of people available to support you. Please ask if you need help, advice or support over the next few days.

REFLECTION POINT

What do you need to do now to ensure that you feel confident should you need to support a bereaved child? Do you need to access additional resources? Do you need to elicit more support from a specialist?

Write a list of tools to support grieving children, which you think might help you at this point in time, and then take some additional time to discuss your ideas with the school's mental health lead and educational psychologist.

References

American Psychiatric Association (APA) (2013) *Diagnostic and Statistical Manual of Mental Disorders* (5th edn). Washington, DC: APA.

Kübler-Ross, E. (1969) *On Death and Dying*. New York, NY: Simon and Schuster.

Stroebe, M. & Schut, H. (1999) 'The dual process model of coping with bereavement: Rationale and description.' *Death Studies, 23*(3), 197–224. doi:10.1080/074811899201046

Tonkin, L. (1996) 'Growing around grief – another way of looking at grief and recovery.' *Bereavement Care, 15*(1), 10.

CHAPTER 11

Eating Disorders

What you need to know

Eating disorders are significant mental health issues involving such behaviours as restricting the amount of food eaten, bingeing and purging, or a combination of these. It is important to remember that eating disorders are not all about the food but about the underlying emotions, and support given by staff in schools should focus on these underlying feelings rather than just the eating behaviour.

REFLECTION POINT

What do you already know about eating disorders? Take some time to consider the statements on the 'Fact or Fiction?' photocopiable handout. The answers are given on another handout on page 194 at the end of this chapter.

✳ EATING DISORDERS: FACT OR FICTION?

1. Most people, at some point in their lives, will feel the need to lose a bit of weight or get fitter.

    ☐ Fiction   ☐ Fact

2. Restricting eating can help people feel more in control.

    ☐ Fiction   ☐ Fact

3. Anyone can develop an eating disorder, although it is most likely to occur in men aged between 15 and 25.

    ☐ Fiction   ☐ Fact

4. Recovery from eating disorders can be quick, if people are given the right help early on.

    ☐ Fiction   ☐ Fact

5. Over 1.2 million people in the UK are affected by an eating disorder.

    ☐ Fiction   ☐ Fact

6. Eating disorders are basically middle-class, attention-seeking behaviour.

    ☐ Fiction   ☐ Fact

7. Girls and women are three times more likely than boys and men to suffer from an eating disorder.

    ☐ Fiction   ☐ Fact

8. Anorexia nervosa has a mortality rate of up to 20 percent, from physical complications and suicide.

    ☐ Fiction   ☐ Fact

What causes eating disorders?

We do not know for certain, but important factors include:

- *Anxiety* – Limiting food can be a way to feel more in control.

- *Longstanding unhappiness* – This may show itself through behaviours around food.

- *Puberty* – Anorexia reverses some of the physical changes of puberty; it might be seen as putting off some of the challenges of becoming an adult.

- *Family* – Saying 'no' to food may be the only way a person can express their feelings.

- *Low self-esteem* – Losing weight may initially help someone to feel more confident and may be accompanied by positive reinforcement regarding their appearance from those around them.

- *Social pressure* – Western culture, particularly the media, idealizes being thin.

- *Genes* – These may play a part.

Types of eating disorders

Table 11.1 gives an overview of the most common eating disorders that you may come across in schools.

Table 11.1 Types of eating disorders

Eating disorder	Description
Anorexia nervosa	Mental health disorder in which people try to attain a very low body weight by restricting food intake, vomiting, using laxatives or excessive exercise. Those with anorexia often see themselves as bigger than they are, so they seek to continue to lose more and more weight.
Bulimia nervosa	Mental health disorder where people feel they have lost control over their eating. This means they often follow a cycle of eating large amounts of food (bingeing), then vomiting, taking laxatives or diuretics (purging) to stop weight gain.

Binge eating disorder (BED)	Mental health disorder where people frequently overeat (binge) and feel that they have no control over their eating. After bingeing, people tend to feel guilt and disgust with themselves.
Avoidant restrictive food intake disorder (ARFID)	A condition in which a person avoids or restricts intake of certain types of food. This is related to several factors, but, most commonly, sensory issues with eating, avoidance following a negative experience (e.g. vomiting, choking) or low interest in food.
Other specified feeding or eating disorder (OSFED)	This diagnosis covers other forms of seriously disordered eating that do not exactly fit the criteria for one of the other diagnoses, for example, those with restricted eating and disordered body image, but of a weight that is considered to be within the normal range.

Signs and symptoms

Anorexia nervosa

The child or young person may show the following signs or symptoms:

- worrying about their appearance and weight
- restricting food intake or eating very slowly
- hiding food
- wearing baggy clothes to conceal weight loss
- only eating very low-calorie food
- fear of high-fat foods
- exercising more
- weight loss.

Bulimia nervosa

The child or young person may show the following signs or symptoms:

- being concerned about their weight or appearance
- bingeing, particularly on high-calorie foods
- mood swings
- disappearing to the toilet during or immediately after eating

- despite frequent purging, they may maintain a normal weight due to the calories absorbed during binges.

How to get help

Depending on the system within your local authority, often school staff or a GP may refer the child or young person to a specialist counsellor, psychiatrist or psychologist. In some cases, a young person can self-refer or be referred for mental health support by their parent or carer.

'I was afraid of getting help. I knew they'd make me eat, and that was terrifying for me at that time.' (Mosi, aged 24)

Treatment for anorexia

- *Talking therapies* – Talking to a psychologist about thoughts and feelings can help the individual to understand how the eating disorder started, and how they can change the ways they think and feel about food and themselves. The psychologist will seek to sensitively support them with ways to cope and build their self-esteem. Talking therapies may include cognitive behavioural therapy (CBT) or adolescent focused psychotherapy.

- *Advice and help with eating* – A dietician may be involved to provide advice about healthy eating and how to safely increase their food intake.

- *Family therapy* – A practitioner may work with the family all together to look at how they can support the young person with their recovery. This may happen with just one family, or sometimes in a group with other young people and their families.

- *Medication* – Medication may be prescribed for other common co-existing mental health needs including OCD, anxiety and depression.

- *Hospital admission* – The child or young person may be required to be admitted into hospital so that their weight can be monitored, and they can receive support to increase their weight if it has reached a dangerously low level.

Treatments for bulimia

- *Cognitive behavioural therapy (CBT)* – CBT helps the young person to explore the links between their thoughts, feelings and actions (see Chapter 7 for more information). The practitioner will encourage them to challenge their thoughts and motivate change.

- *Family therapy* – This involves the individual and their family meeting with a therapist to talk about how the bulimia has impacted on the young person, and how the family can work together to support them.

REFLECTION POINT
Think about your own relationship to food. Have you ever restricted your eating? How and why? What was your objective? How did this behaviour affect others in your family or friendship group? Do you think most people will have had some issues around their eating patterns in their lives? If so, why?

CASE STUDY
Heidi was in Year 9. Marlowe, a teaching assistant, had noticed that Heidi was looking very thin and pale. She often wanted to keep her coat on during lessons, saying that she was too cold. At lunchtimes, Heidi never went into the dinner hall, and all Marlowe had seen her eat was a rice cake; it had taken her the whole lunch hour to eat it, as she had nibbled on it so slowly. Marlowe thought perhaps Heidi was physically unwell at first, but when she overheard Heidi saying that she wanted to lose weight, Marlowe became worried that Heidi was dangerously and purposefully restricting her calorie intake.

Marlowe reported her concerns to the DSL and MHL, and they agreed that Marlowe should speak to Heidi. She was careful not to approach Heidi during a lunchtime. She asked Heidi how she was feeling, rather than commenting on anything to do with her weight or appearance. At first, Heidi said that she was fine, and didn't want to talk. The DSL spoke to Heidi's parents to check how she had been at home and whether they had any concerns. They were desperately worried about Heidi and admitted that they had caught her lying about how much she was eating on several occasions. Heidi's friends were also worried and confronted her about it. Heidi became very defensive, which led her to fall out with some of her closest friends, leaving Heidi feeling isolated and alone.

Marlowe checked in on Heidi again, and she admitted that she was feeling out of control. She said that she hated herself, calling herself 'fat' and 'ugly'. She admitted that she was barely eating, but begged Marlowe not to tell anyone. Marlowe explained that she had a duty of care to get her some help and reassured her that she would be there to help her on the road to recovery. Marlowe explained that there were support groups of other young people who felt the same, and she put her in touch with them. She also sought a referral to the Eating Disorders Team at CAMHS and helped Heidi to mend her relationships.

Questions

1. What signs do you think Marlowe noticed that made her concerned?

2. Why was it important that Marlowe did not try to have a conversation with Heidi at lunchtime?

3. Why do you think that Marlowe was careful to focus on feelings rather than Heidi's appearance?

Body image: What you need to know

Body image has a direct link to the development of eating disorders in some children and young people. It is, again, very important for those working with children and young people to have an understanding of body image and of how to specifically challenge negative and unhelpful thinking and behaviours around this issue.

A *positive body image* means (adapted from Collins-Donnelly, 2014):

• being content with your body

• feeling comfortable with your body

- feeling satisfied with how you look

- realizing that the *perfect* body does not exist

- recognizing that who you are as a person is more important than how you look

- knowing that the health of your body is more important than how it looks

- learning to appreciate your body and what it can do for you.

Attitudes to body image

In 2013, the UK government's British Social Attitudes Survey (BSAS) explored the way in which adults viewed their bodies. They found that a proportion of both men and women are dissatisfied with their body image – women more so than men (63 percent of women were satisfied compared with 74 percent of men) – and dissatisfaction with body image remained constant in people's lives, meaning that, for example, a woman in her fifties was as likely to be as dissatisfied with her body image as her teenage daughter (NatCen Social Research, 2013).

The BSAS highlighted that 77 percent of adults felt society places too much pressure on women to have a sexualized appearance; while the Girls' Attitudes Survey (Girlguiding, 2016), harnessing the opinions of over 1600 girls and young women aged 7 to 21, reported that girls as young as seven felt the impact of images in the media.

Many of the men and women questioned in the BSAS agreed that 'how you look affects what you can achieve in life'. Unfortunately, this is not just the case for adults. Within the Girls' Attitudes Survey, almost half (47%) of 11- to 21-year-olds felt that the way they looked held them back. Over half of girls and a quarter of boys think that their peers have body-image problems. The survey found that girls as young as age five are worried about being fat. One in four 7-year-old girls have tried to lose weight at least once. One third of boys aged 8 to 12 years diet to lose weight (YMCA, 2012).

Body image isn't just a problem for girls. Of one thousand 8- to 18-year-old boys surveyed by Credos (2016), 55 percent said they would change their diet to improve their appearance, and 23 percent believed the 'perfect male body' exists.

'I started going to the gym and drinking protein shakes when I was 16. I don't want to be the skinny kid with no muscles.' (Zahir, aged 18)

REFLECTION POINT
Think about your own body image. When you look in the mirror, what are the first thoughts that pop into your head about how you look? Would you regard yourself as having a positive body image? Do you think it is important to model this to children and young people that you support – especially those with disordered eating or body-image issues?

The link to self-esteem

Our self-esteem, the way in which we feel about ourselves, can vary across the lifespan, particularly following major life changes. Given that adolescence is a time of rapid change and transformation, both on the inside and outside, it can lead children and young people to feel negatively about themselves and their bodies.

Whilst not every young person with low self-esteem will develop an eating disorder, research indicates a strong correlation between negative body image, low self-esteem and the development of eating disorders. For example, Mallaram et al. (2023) found that young people who are dissatisfied with their bodies are more likely to engage in disordered eating behaviours to cope with their feelings.

In our view, therefore, tackling the issues related to body image and self-esteem among young people needs to be central to the wellbeing curriculum in our schools.

'I know that I don't look like the girls I follow on social media, but I'm okay with that.' (Grace, aged 17)

REFLECTION POINT
Think about how you currently support children and young people to maintain a healthy level of self-esteem. What strategies do you use? Make a list and discuss this with colleagues to

identify any similarities in your approaches, but also to consider any alternatives that work for others.

Top tips and strategies

As with all mental health issues, our FIRES acronym can help you to respond safely and effectively. Chapter 1 gives a full description of each stage, but Table 11.2 gives some specific key points to consider if you are concerned that a child may have an eating disorder.

Table 11.2 FIRES and eating disorders

F	Fast response	Avoid approaching the young person at mealtimes. Focus on feelings and behaviours and not on weight, food or appearance.
I	Identify needs and risks	Is there a medical emergency – for example, fainting or a racing heart? Clarify any issues regarding self-harm, anxiety, low mood or suicidal thoughts.
R	Reassure	Aim to support the young person to feel safe enough to seek help or support.
E	Empathize and listen	Stay calm, even if the young person becomes defensive or angry. Do not try to force change but make them aware that support is available and how and where they can access it.
S	Support and signpost	Share your concerns with the designated safeguarding lead, mental health lead, parents and carers where possible, and refer to CAMHS for early intervention.

Support and signpost

There is a range of key tools and strategies that you can help the child or young person to access independently of your support. As with any other mental health issue, it is important to encourage the individual to seek support via a range of different means in order to build up their own set of self-help strategies.

The following can be useful for those with eating disorders:

• making use of CBT self-help booklets

• avoiding the use of alcohol and drugs

- increasing the range of self-help strategies for comorbidities

- encouraging communication with family and friends

- participation in relevant support groups and networks (see the 'Where to Get More Help' section).

Tips on promoting a healthy body image

We would want to help all young people to develop a positive body image. MacConville (2019) summarizes the *characteristics of positive body image* as follows:

- Body appreciation

  - appreciating the health of the body

  - appreciating the body for what it can do more than for its appearance

  - expressing comfort with and love for the body, despite not being completely satisfied with all its aspects

  - choosing to focus on body assets rather than perceived body flaws

  - avoiding potentially hazardous ways to alter appearance (e.g. strict dieting, over-exercising, cosmetic surgery)

- Optimism and a positive outlook

  - feeling that our inner qualities 'shine through' and boost one's appearance and behaviour

  - feeling good about oneself, being optimistic and happy, which shows up as helping others, smiling, asserting oneself, holding one's head up high, standing tall and conveying confidence and wellbeing

- Broad conception of beauty

  - viewing a wide range of weights, shapes and appearances as beautiful

  - believing that what makes people beautiful is carrying the self well, e.g. being groomed and confident rather than conforming to a media ideal

- Media literate

    - being aware that many media messages are unrealistic

    - rejecting and/or challenging media images such as of ultra-thin models and/or negative comments about our appearance that could undermine and damage our body image on a regular basis

- Unconditional acceptance from others

    - recognizing body acceptance from others (e.g. family, friends)

    - feeling loved, special and valued for who we are and our character strengths rather than for our appearance (when one's appearance is mentioned by others, comments are usually complimentary and related to aspects within one's control, e.g. clothes, grooming, hairstyle)

- Listening to and taking care of the body

    - taking part in enjoyable activities and exercise

    - having regular check-ups and seeking advice when unwell

    - looking after the body, developing healthy habits

    - trusting the body to know when and how much to eat, eating a variety of foods that are enjoyable, healthy and keep the body performing well.

REFLECTION POINT

Take some time to consider these characteristics in turn. Think about what you can do in your role to support a child or young person in each area. What tools and strategies do you currently have at your disposal? What might you need to develop further? Where can you gain some additional support and help if you feel the right kind of resources are not available to you at this current time? It is important to remember how this topic is taught within the curriculum in your school and the way in which the staff are trained to support and nurture children in this area. There needs to be a consistent approach on an individual, group and whole-school level, and you need to be very clear about what your role is within such an approach. Take some time to discuss this with colleagues and your line manager to ensure that you are offering support that is consistent with the whole-school ethos and approach.

In your role supporting young people, it is important that you are fully aware of your own ability to appreciate the way that you look and how you feel about your body. This is vital because, as the adult in the relationship, children and young people look to us for advice and support but also, essentially, to learn how to respond themselves. We, therefore, have to be positive role models in this area by promoting a healthy attitude to body image ourselves. This involves the following basic strategies:

- Avoid making comments about your own or another person's body size and shape, even if the comment is positive. Complimenting someone by saying that they have lost weight can be just as damaging to their self-esteem as making a comment that is meant in a more derogatory way. Try instead to praise their strengths, talents and character traits, rather than focusing upon their appearance.

- Incorporate media literacy lessons into the curriculum so that children and young people are reminded that the images they see in the media are not always what they seem – many have been digitally altered, filtered and taken with lighting to portray a flawless and 'perfect' appearance.

- Encourage children and young people to eat a healthy balanced diet with the aim of being healthy and strong, rather than focusing upon trying to appear a certain way. Avoid referring to 'good food' or 'bad food', as most foods are fine in moderation and as part of a healthy, balanced diet.

'I was desperate to be thin and kept following silly diets. I gave up bread, pasta, crisps, biscuits, sugar, cheese... I lost weight, but I was miserable, weak and not much fun to be around! It definitely did not make people like me more, and I still didn't feel good about myself. I thought if I lost weight everything would be better, but it wasn't.'
(Maria, ex-pupil, aged 20)

References

Collins-Donnelly, K. (2014) *Banish Your Body Image Thief.* London: Jessica Kingsley Publishers.

Credos (2016) Picture of health? https://adassoc.org.uk/credos/picture-of-health

Girlguiding (2016) *Girls' Attitudes Survey 2016.* www.girlguiding.org.uk/globalassets/docs-and-resources/research-and-campaigns/girls-attitudes-survey-2016.pdf

MacConville, R. (2019) *Positive Body Image in the Early Years: A Practical Guide.* London: Jessica Kingsley Publishers.

Mallaram, G.K., Sharma, P., Kattula, D., Singh, S. & Pavuluru, P. (2023) 'Body image perception, eating disorder behavior, self-esteem and quality of life: A cross-sectional study among female medical students.' *Journal of Eating Disorders, 11*(225). doi:10.1186/s40337-023-00945-2

NatCen Social Research (2013) *British Social Attitudes 30.* https://natcen.ac.uk/publications/british-social-attitudes-30

YMCA (2012) *Reflections on Body Image: All Party Parliamentary Group on Body Image.* http://ymca-central-assets.s3-eu-west-1.amazonaws.com/s3fs-public/APPG-Reflections-on-body-image.pdf

✳ EATING DISORDERS: THE FACTS

1. This is true. Many people will feel the need or urge to get fitter or slimmer, which is often a healthy response to maintain overall wellbeing.

2. This is true. Often a person feels that they have very little control over events around them, and restricting their food intake can help them feel more in control. This is one of the reasons cited for the increase in eating disorders during the pandemic.

3. This is false. People from all demographics can develop an eating disorder, but it is most likely to occur in young women aged between 15 and 25.

4. This is false. Recovering from an eating disorder can take a long time, and it is common for a person to experience setbacks before making a full recovery.

5. This is true.

6. This is false. Anyone from any walk of life can be vulnerable, and these disorders are very complicated and go across class and cultural backgrounds.

7. This is true. Unfortunately, girls and young women are more vulnerable to eating disorders. However, there is also evidence that boys are increasingly at risk of experiencing an eating disorder.

8. This is true and one of the reasons why this disorder needs to be taken seriously and meaningfully addressed with young people. Eating disorders can kill.

CHAPTER 12

Emotionally Based School Avoidance (EBSA)

What is EBSA?

Many children, at some time in their school career, are challenged by anxiety or other overwhelming emotions that make it very difficult for them to attend school. While considering this group, it is important that we are 'distinguishing these children who cannot attend from those truants who *will not* attend' (Thambirajah, Grandison & De-Hayes, 2007, p.16).

The language we use really does matter, as the words reflect the lens through which we see the behaviour and the words or attitudes others are then invited to use or adopt. School 'refusal' strongly implies that the behaviour is 'deliberate' or 'chosen', which has significant implications for possible responses, suggesting or potentially prompting those which may be punitive in nature.

Most of the current literature refers to 'phobia' and 'refusal' – bear this in mind. Many writers may be quoting this term due to the literature they have read. Our preferred terminology is either 'emotionally based school avoidance' (EBSA) or 'emotionally based school non-attendance' (EBSNA). In our view, EBSA most accurately describes the issue, as many children continue to attend school despite showing other avoidant behaviours, such as being very reluctant to attend and needing significant support from parents and school staff to transition into school each morning and stay throughout the school day. The term EBSA promotes early intervention before non-attendance becomes entrenched.

All school staff need to be aware of EBSA, its causes and the evidence-based approaches to supporting children who experience it. Children who are anxious about attending school will often need the help of a safe, supportive, consistent and predictable adult to help them transition back into the school environment gradually.

REFLECTION POINT

Think about a specific child or young person that you have worked with who has found it difficult to come into school on a daily basis. Try to think about where their anxiety came from in the first place, and why it escalated in the way that it did. Take some time to write a list of all the factors that may have contributed to the child or young person not wanting to attend school. Think about the following key areas which may have impacted on the young person:

- workload

- parental wellbeing

- peer group/bullying

- loss or bereavement

- special educational need

- mental health issues

- financial hardship

- looked after status

- transition.

You may well think of other factors, too, but this activity aims to highlight the complexity of this issue.

'Florence was so anxious about school. She has autism and everything about secondary school was too much for her – the crowds, the noise, the changes of staff, the transitions. She just couldn't cope.' (*parent of child with EBSA*)

In 2015, the UK literature suggested that approximately 1 and 2 percent of the school population, with a slightly higher prevalence among secondary school students, were absent from school for emotional reasons (Gulliford & Miller, 2015). However, persistent absence rates in the UK have soared since the pandemic. Recent statistics released by the government reported that in the autumn term 2019/2020, 13.1 percent of children were persistently absent from school (i.e. less than 90% attendance). In the autumn term 2022/23, that figure had increased to a staggering 24.2 percent (House of Commons Library, 2023). While not all of these persistent absences are related to emotionally based school avoidance, in our experience, many schools have seen a marked increase in this since the pandemic.

Early identification and support for young people at risk of EBSA can be challenging due to the difficulties children face in expressing their distress and the challenges that parents and school staff encounter in understanding pupils' experience of school. These factors often act as key barriers in the process (Thambirajah et al., 2007). There are some key differences in the ways in which the distress young people experience is displayed. It will be very obvious for some, as their non-attendance will be chronic. Others may have more variable attendance, missing occasional days or lessons, or only attending school when provided with a modified timetable and high level of adult support.

The onset of EBSA can occur suddenly or gradually, with peaks in behaviours linked to school phase transitions, such as moving from primary to secondary school (King & Bernstein, 2001). A report by ImpactEd (2024) also highlighted increased risk at the transition between Years 7 and 8.

There are groups of children and young people with medical conditions such as autistic spectrum disorder (ASD) and attention deficit and hyperactivity disorder (ADHD) who will be more at risk of developing emotionally based school avoidance, and they will need a more bespoke and differentiated intervention. For example, teaching children with ASD relaxing techniques such as mindfulness – particularly in the whole-class context – can increase their levels of anxiety. Often, there will need to be a focus on creating an environment that is less overwhelming to the senses and features fewer transitions, a clear structure and routine and fewer social demands.

How does EBSA start and develop?

Starting school can be a frightening experience for young children. It is often the first time they will be away from their parents for an extended time, and this can make them feel anxious and worried. They might also feel tired and overwhelmed by the new routine of school, making them feel even more vulnerable.

Even for older children who are already familiar with the school environment, returning to school after the long summer break or an extended absence due to illness can be a challenging experience. They may experience a sense of displacement and disorientation, as their social circle and classroom may have changed. Additionally, they may have grown accustomed to the comfort and security of being at home and may feel vulnerable and exposed when they return to the school setting. Some children may also develop a fear of school-related triggers, such as the school bus or the classroom, due to previous negative experiences, which can lead to further anxiety and avoidance behaviours.

We all tend to avoid situations that make us anxious, but sadly, these behaviours can become a routine and form habits that can be hard to break. Avoidance is a very natural and understandable protective response to a frightening situation. This avoidance brings instant relief; however, in the long-term, avoidance often heightens the anxiety. At the outset, it is vital to identify possible triggers for the emotionally based school avoidance, prior to analysing them and putting in place an intervention to support the child to reintegrate into the school over time gradually. Possible *triggers for EBSA* include:

- experiencing bullying

- starting school

- moving to a school

- having an extended absence from school due to illness or holiday

- a bereavement

- a change in the family, such as the birth of a new baby

- having a traumatic experience

- conflict or violence at home, including exposure to arguments, separation and divorce, witnessing domestic abuse

- experiencing abuse

- friendship issues

- learning difficulties.

'Milly was struggling with reading, and it made her really hate being at school. Her self-esteem was so low, and being in lessons, feeling like she was always failing, was torture for her. She was sick with worry every morning, and I couldn't get her in. Then the more she missed, the more anxious she was about going back.' (parent of child with EBSA)

Risk factors

Research suggests that there are some factors that place children and young people at higher risk of emotionally based school avoidance:

- Child factors

  - temperamental style – reluctance to interact and withdrawal from unfamiliar settings, people or objects

  - fear of failure and poor self-confidence

  - physical illness

  - age (5–6, 11–12 and 13–14 years)

  - learning difficulties, developmental problems or autism spectrum condition if unidentified or unsupported

  - separation anxiety from parent

  - traumatic events

- Family factors

  - separation and divorce or change in family dynamic

  - parent physical and mental health problems

  - overprotective parenting style

  - dysfunctional family interactions

  - being the youngest child in the family

- loss and bereavement
- high levels of family stress
- family history of young carer
- School factors
  - bullying (the most common school factor)
  - difficulties in specific subject
  - transition to secondary school, key stage or change of school
  - structure of the school day
  - academic demands
  - transport or journey to school
  - exams
  - peer or staff relationship difficulties.

In addition, there are emotional and behavioural signs that may indicate that a child is at risk of EBSA:

- increase in anxiety
- declining punctuality
- negative talk about school
- reduced engagement in the school context
- atypical behaviour
- displays of anger, anxiety or stress.

Top tips and strategies
Assess, plan, do and review

Using an 'Assess, Plan, Do, Review' approach is generally considered to be best practice in supporting children and young people suffering with emotionally based school avoidance.

To fully understand the child or young person, it is vital to discuss all the aspects at play, incorporating the views of everyone involved. This includes the child at the outset, their parents or carers, and staff and peers with whom they interact on a daily basis. Once this information has been gathered, a realistic reintegration plan can be developed. This should always be done in a very systematic and step-by-step way. It is important to avoid 'flooding' by pushing the child too quickly or too soon. This can be entirely counter-productive and reinforce heightened levels of anxiety. A 'tough love' or forceful approach is very rarely successful.

Ensuring that all the resources are in place, and that communication systems between school and home are healthy, is also essential if the plan is ultimately to work; monitoring progress on setting reviews is also necessary. It is important to consider your specific role in this whole process and how you can and should advocate for the child and family, while also ensuring that the plan is disseminated appropriately for all who are supporting the child in the school context.

Identification and assessment: Working with the young person

Whatever the child's age, it is crucial to provide them with the opportunity to express their views and ideas about the difficulties they are experiencing and what they feel would be helpful. The approach taken will depend on the child's chronological age, level of understanding and language, and preferred method of expression. A key part of any work with a young person experiencing EBSA will be for the adult to listen and provide an empathetic response.

Younger children often find it difficult to describe their feelings, so a creative art- or play-based approach may be more helpful. For instance, drawing a picture to *show* their feelings may be less intimidating than answering lots of questions. Being invited to draw a picture of their school or classroom might be a starting point in exploring an individual's experiences of school, both positive and negative.

Older children and teenagers may be more comfortable conversing about their experiences. Ideally, this needs to take place with an adult that the child feels that they have a good relationship with and that they can trust. If the young person is not attending school, careful consideration needs to be given to where the conversation might occur. For both children and young people, using sorting activities can help support them in identifying triggers for their anxiety and thinking about strategies that they might find helpful.

A planned return

Once an assessment has been completed, a plan should be drawn up with parents, school staff and any other agencies involved. A meeting may take place at school, in the home or at another setting within the community to allow the young person to participate. The young person's views should be included in the planning, even if they do not feel that they are able to attend the meeting.

At this stage, depending on the level of anxiety the young person is displaying and the length of time they have been out of school, the following possibilities should be considered:

- a return to school on a full timetable

- implementation of a part-time timetable with a gradual return

- consultation with CAMHS and other agencies, which may, if necessary, lead to a referral for out-of-school tuition as part of a reintegration plan

- a period of recovery that may be needed before the pupil can return to any form of education.

As part of the reintegration process, it might be helpful to discuss the following with the child or young person:

- where they are most comfortable sitting in class

- which teachers and members of staff they feel most comfortable with

- how they find it easiest to enter the room

- who will support them

- whether or not they can cope with being asked questions in class

- how they get from class to class

- where they feel comfortable in school if they can't get into class

- whether they feel comfortable using the school toilets

- how they feel about being in the dinner hall

- how they feel about unstructured time (e.g. before school, break and lunchtime).

CASE STUDY

Matilda, aged 9, was experiencing anxiety about separating from her mother and coming into school, following a series of traumatic events, including the death of her father after a long illness. Matilda was terrified of being away from her mother, who was suffering with her own mental health difficulties. Keith (the emotional literacy support assistant) had a good relationship with Matilda. On a day when Matilda was able to come in for a few hours, Keith took the opportunity to speak to her about how she was feeling.

Keith knew that Matilda would find it difficult to express her feelings verbally, so he brought some emotion cards with him and some sorting cards labelled with different activities that Matilda does at school (e.g. Maths, Break Time, Answering Questions, Reading Aloud, etc.). Matilda was able to express that she felt worried when she had to do writing or reading aloud and at lunchtime in the dinner hall. They used this activity as the basis for a conversation about what might help Matilda, including having lunch with a friend in a quiet classroom, not being asked to read aloud in front of the class unless she volunteered, and having alternative ways to record information.

Together they completed a support plan, and the discussion with Matilda formed the basis of a plan that was then agreed with the MHL, class teacher and Matilda's mum. It was agreed that, initially, Matilda would come in for part days, and gradually extend the time that she was in school. Part of the plan involved Keith meeting Matilda from her car and having a 10-minute check in with her, where they did a consistent, predictable, calming activity so that Matilda could feel safe and settled before going to class. Within two weeks, Matilda was back in school full-time, feeling much less anxious and immensely proud of what she had achieved.

Questions

1. What resources do you have in school to gain a young person's views if you feel that talking about their feelings might be difficult?

2. What factors in this case do you think led to the success of the reintegration?

3. What support do you think Matilda may need in the longer term to support her emotional needs?

Strategies you can use with a child or young person

In your role, you may be tasked with gaining the views of the child or young person, and the following strategies may be helpful to you:

1. Ask the child to think about their thoughts and feelings about school, and what these would look like if they could be drawn.

   - What name would they give the feeling that they experience when they think about going to school?

   - If it was a thing, what would it look like? What would it say?

   - How does the [...] get in the way of them attending school? When is [...] in charge, and when are they in charge?

2. Ask them to draw how their body feels when they are worried.

3. Use an anxiety thermometer, ladder or scale to ask the child what aspects of school they find difficult; some areas to consider include:

   - the physical environment (e.g. toilets, corridors, assembly hall)

   - times of the day or social interactions (e.g. arriving at school, play and breaktimes, lining up to go into school or classroom, lunchtimes, going home, changing for PE)

   - particular lessons or activities within lessons (e.g. writing, working as part of a group, reading aloud, verbally answering a question).

4. A life graph can also help them tell you their 'story so far' and what they would want in the future.

Developing support plans for those returning to school

The photocopiable framework on pages 206–7 can help with developing a plan by identifying the support systems for the individual child or young person.

References

Gulliford, A. & Miller, A. (2015) 'Coping with Life by Coping with School? School Refusal in Young People.' In T. Cline, A. Gulliford & S. Birch (Eds.), *Educational Psychology* (pp.258–282). London: Routledge.

House of Commons Library (2023) *School Attendance in England: Research Briefing.* https://researchbriefings.files.parliament.uk/documents/CBP-9710/CBP-9710.pdf

ImpactEd (2024) *Understanding Attendance: Findings on the Drivers of Pupil Absence from over 30,000 Young People in England.* www.evaluation.impactedgroup.uk/research-and-resources/understanding-attendance

King, N.J. & Bernstein, G.A. (2001) 'School refusal in children and adolescents: A review of the past 10 years.' *Journal of American Academic Child Adolescent Psychiatry, 40*(2), 97–205.

Thambirajah, M.S., Grandison, K.J. & De-Hayes, L. (2007) *Understanding School Refusal: A Handbook for Professionals in Education, Health and Social Care.* London: Jessica Kingsley Publishers.

✳ SUPPORT PLAN

Name .... Date ....

At school, these things can make me feel upset:

My school support person(s) is/are:
Details of checking in with my school support person (when, where)

Until .... my return-to-school plan includes the following changes to my attendance:
(Identify any changes to days or time they come in)

Changes to my timetable include:
(Identify any changes needed and what should happen/where they should go instead)

Any other changes include:
(Identify any other changes to routines (break, lunchtimes, changes between lessons, etc.) to classroom expectations (not expected to read aloud, work in pairs, etc.) homework)

When I start to get upset, I notice these things about myself:

When I start to get upset, others notice these things about me:

Things I can do to make myself feel better when I'm at school:

Things that other people (staff and friends) can do to help me feel better when I'm at school:

Things that my family can do to support me to attend school:

Places in school where I can go to feel safe and supported:

This plan will be reviewed regularly so that it remains helpful.

Review date: ....

My signature	School support person's signature	Parent signature
....	....	....

■ CHAPTER 13 ■

Suicide

Suicide and self-harm in young people
Millennium Cohort Study

The Millennium Cohort Study, which followed the lives of approximately 19,000 young people born at the start of the millennium in England, Scotland, Wales and Northern Ireland, found that, by 17 years old, about 7 percent of these children had attempted suicide. Almost one in four said they had self-harmed (Patalay & Fitzsimons, 2020).

Such statistics are clearly shocking and distressing for adults who are seeking to ensure that our children and young people's wellbeing and mental health is protected and fostered. The data, which is nationally representative, can be extrapolated to the UK population to give figures of 52,427 17-year-olds having attempted suicide at some point in their lives, and 170,744 having self-harmed in the previous 12 months before the pandemic hit.

Sadly, it has become increasingly evident that the pandemic and its fallout will probably make matters worse for many years to come, and this suggests a real need to ensure that children can access specialist clinical support and services at the earliest opportunity. For many in the psychological services, there is a recognition that more support is necessary, that the services are underfunded, and that there is a need to provide earlier, more and better support for young people to prevent their difficulties getting so severe that they consider suicide. However, we also need to be more aware of the specific reasons why children and young people appear to be suffering to such a great extent at this current time.

Highlighting inequalities

The Millennium Cohort Study also highlighted large inequalities in these adverse mental health outcomes at the age of 17, with women and sexual minorities being particularly vulnerable, potentially reflecting the greater disparity in the pressures that they face and highlighting the need for support that is sensitive to the challenges experienced during adolescence.

The study also highlighted that austerity and poverty clearly led to more people experiencing difficulties. Another key issue is that of education, which continues to cause huge amounts of stress to many teenagers in particular.

While we know that it is really important that all children are able to thrive in the education system, many do not access university or higher education. It is also a given fact that, within this group, many of these children and young people have learning difficulties or autism or suffer from traumatic experiences. There is also a direct link to those who are looked after by local authority social services.

Falling through the gap

The report emphasized the significance of the age of 17. Young people transfer from child and adolescent mental health services (CAMHS) to adult services from the age of 18, leaving them vulnerable to falling through the gap at this crucial stage. This gap in support can have a negative impact on their mental health outcomes. These findings highlight the pressing need for urgent mental health support for this generation.

It is, therefore, so important that mental health support is available at the school-based level. Key to this is the mental health lead, but also those taking on supportive roles in providing therapeutic support in schools for our most vulnerable children and young people.

Support in schools

Many school-based staff voice concerns about how they could or should respond to a child who is experiencing suicidal thoughts. In research carried out by suicide-prevention charity Papyrus (2018), approximately 11 percent of school staff said that students share such thoughts with them at least once each term. However, only 53 percent of this number said that they felt confident in saying or doing the right thing in response. Concerns shared in the research include:

- feeling responsible and possibly being left to 'carry the can' if something happened

- feeling unsure as to whether the disclosure was attention-seeking rather than genuine thoughts of suicide

- concerns that there are problems getting senior teachers to take notice

- feeling that there is a lack of time to spend with the student or young person in order to discuss their concerns

- feeling worried about gaining the right kind of support from the management team and concerned about fulfilling other roles and responsibilities to others in the class or form group

- wanting to help but not feeling qualified to do so.

When considering this very triggering and complex issue, it is important that you are aware of your own views and acknowledge and understand your emotional responses. This is particularly important if you have experienced suicide in your own family or friendship group.

REFLECTION POINT
Take some time to reflect on your own experiences and how you may have accessed appropriate support. Try to identify your own worries about supporting children and young people in this area. It can be helpful to make a list of these and to discuss them with your line manager. This is an extremely important task as you need to feel confident that you are doing no harm in your interactions with vulnerable children and young people, while also supporting them in the most appropriate way and signposting them to the relevant support services that can help prevent the escalation of their difficulties and anxieties.

What you need to know
Risk factors

Suicide is *preventable*. Young people who are thinking of ending their lives often give warning signs of their emotional distress. Recognizing the risk factors and warning signs of suicide and knowing how to respond can help prevent it.

No child is immune to the risk of suicide, but there are common factors that can increase the chances of having suicidal thoughts (see Table 13.1).

Table 13.1 Suicide risk factors

Environmental	Family	Individual
Exam pressure	Being in the care system	Having social, emotional or mental health needs
Bullying	Domestic violence	
Being in the youth justice system	Family breakdown	Alcohol or drugs misuse
Media reports of suicide	Bereavement	Physical or sexual abuse
	Suicide of a family member or friend	Sexual orientation/ gender identity
	Being a young carer	Feeling isolated
	Conflict with family or friends	Self-harm

CASE STUDY

Yasmina (Year 12) had been struggling with low mood on and off for several years. She had been prescribed antidepressants and had undertaken counselling the previous year, both of which seemed to have helped to lift her. However, recently, Yasmina had been feeling very low again. She had made comments about hating her life and wanting to die, but her parents put it down to 'typical teenage angst'. Over the last few months, Yasmina had spent more time in her room and on her computer, and less time with her friends, which worried her parents. When, one day, Yasmina woke up seeming more motivated, her parents were delighted. They were even more pleased, albeit surprised, when Yasmina had tidied her room and was taking a large bag to the charity shop. They hoped that Yasmina was finally coming out of her dark spell and was in the midst of a fresh new beginning.

Questions

1. What were the warning signs that Yasmina may be at risk of suicide?

2. What could be another explanation for Yasmina taking a large bag to the charity shop, other than wanting a fresh start? Why might that be a warning sign?

What to look out for

According to research, feelings of entrapment and hopelessness are the most common experiences of those who are feeling suicidal (O'Connor, 2021). However, signs that something is wrong can sometimes be more difficult to spot. For example, the young person might display a cheeriness that may seem fake to you, or they may joke about their emotions, saying something quite alarming but disguised as a joke. Don't ignore your gut feeling if you are concerned about a child. Some children won't be open about how they are feeling. Equally, suddenly becoming calm after a period of depression or irritability can be a sign that the child has decided to end their life.

Some children will show their distress outwardly, but many will internalize how they are feeling for fear of how others may react to their frightening thoughts. When thinking about what will happen after they are gone, children and young people may give their favourite toys and possessions away, or they may talk about splitting the toys up among the people they know. They may also navigate their intense emotions by drawing pictures or writing stories that depict suicide. They may talk about their feelings of hopelessness or how they are a burden to others.

We must familiarize ourselves with the common signs of suicide ideation in our young people, but note that it can display more subtly in younger children. Regardless of a child's age, however, it is important to never take any warning signs lightly.

'It is so hard to hear a six-year-old saying that they wish they'd never been born.' (Sarah, teacher)

The most common observable signs of suicidal thoughts are :

- talking about wanting to die (or drawing out, play-acting/pretending death or suicide) or making plans for suicide

- displaying severe emotional pain or distress

- feelings of hopelessness

- talking about being a burden (or not belonging in the world/family/community/school, etc.)

- withdrawing from family, friends and previously enjoyed activities

- behaviour that is out of character (repeated anger, aggressiveness, hostility or recklessness)

- problems in school (poor grades, missed classes, inappropriate behaviour)

- increased risk-taking behaviours (vandalism, promiscuous sex, substance abuse).

Top tips and strategies
Build relationships and open communication

A child or young person who is thinking about suicide may not feel able to access the support of those around them. They may be afraid, believing that those around them don't care, feeling a sense of shame or embarrassment, or because they fear sharing whatever is causing their thoughts of suicide. It is important to provide safe spaces and frequent opportunities for children to talk about how they are feeling, and to create an environment and ethos in your school where children feel that they can talk to you about anything without judgement.

Asking is key

Research indicates that asking someone if they are feeling suicidal can protect them. It allows them to feel connected, listened to and cared for. Many people worry that raising the discussion will endanger the young person, but you might actually be saving their life (O'Connor, 2021).

We must not be afraid to break down the taboo and help a young person to feel safe enough to talk to us about suicide. If they open up, it is so much easier for us to intervene.

Useful/helpful language

When we talk about suicide, we need to be mindful of language that is helpful and unhelpful. According to Papyrus (2018), there are some common phrases in our vocabulary that we need to watch out for as they can be unhelpful and offensive.

- 'Commit' suicide originates from when suicide was seen as a criminal act. This law was changed in 1961, but unfortunately, this continues to be a commonly used phrase. It is better to use phrases such as 'taken their own life' or 'died by suicide'.

- Avoid using vague language such as, 'You're not thinking about doing something stupid, are you?' This insinuates that the young person might be 'stupid' for having thoughts of suicide and make them feel less able to open up. Unless you use clear, unambiguous language, you cannot be sure of how they're feeling. Papyrus (2018) suggest that it is better to use phrases such as, 'Are you telling me that you are thinking of taking your own life/suicide?'

- Don't use the words 'successful' or 'unsuccessful'/'failed' to describe a suicide attempt.

Remove opportunities for harm

It is important to ensure that the physical environment of your school or college is as safe as possible, for example, ensuring that students do not have access to areas from which they could jump, ensuring that any harmful substances are locked away, and removing possible ligature points. A risk assessment and 'suicide safer strategy' will be necessary to develop in any school context.

REFLECTION POINT

Find out about your school's policy in this area. It is very important that you fully understand how to support the development of a risk assessment for individual children and young people, and how these fit with the whole-school policy and protocols. Talk to the designated safeguarding lead and school's mental health lead to gain the most accurate picture and ensure that you are following the protocols as agreed by the staff team as a whole.

Supporting a child who is having suicidal thoughts: Key points

The FIRES Framework described in Chapter 1 will help you to respond safely and effectively to a young person expressing suicidal thoughts. For a full description of each stage, refer to Chapter 1. With regard to children experiencing suicidal thoughts, Table 13.2 shows some further points to consider.

Table 13.2 FIRES and suicide risk

F	Fast response	Always call 999 immediately and inform all relevant staff and parents should a child present as immediately at risk of suicide.
I	Identify needs and risks	Assess whether the young person is at immediate risk of suicide. If they refuse to talk to you then find someone they will talk to. If you think the young person may be a risk to themselves, stay with them and do not leave them.
R	Reassure	Show them that you can handle their frightening feelings and do not dismiss them, while also being very clear that there is always hope.
E	Empathize and listen	Listen and avoid using guilt as a motivator. Help them to identify sources of support and hope.
S	Support and signpost	Support them to make a safety plan (see Chapter 7 for an example) and refer to the designated safeguarding lead, mental health lead, parents and carers where possible, and seek an urgent referral via the GP or by dialling 111 or your local CAMHS crisis line.

CASE STUDY

Oonagh had been suffering with anxiety and depression throughout her time at secondary school and had confided in a friend that she was going to end her life. Thankfully, Oonagh's friend told the head of year, who took fast and appropriate action, and Oonagh started to receive therapeutic support from CAMHS.

Erin, a teaching assistant, developed a rapport with Oonagh so that she knew that she had a key person to talk to within school. One of the activities that Erin did with Oonagh was to put together a safety plan. The purpose was to make sure that Oonagh had strategies planned for if she ever felt suicidal again. They made a list of helpline numbers that Oonagh could call, and whom she could speak to at home, in school and in the middle of the night. They also wrote a plan of things that Oonagh could do to make herself feel happier and give herself some hope. As part of this, they made a playlist of songs that Oonagh liked and also made an album of photos on her phone that reminded her of how much she was loved. Erin gave Oonagh a journal in which she could write down her thoughts; she gave Oonagh the option to share this with her whenever she wanted to so that they could talk through some of the feelings and review them. This helped Oonagh to see that some of her dark thoughts and feelings were temporary and fleeting. Oonagh saved the safety plan on her phone so that she always had it with her.

Questions

1. What could you do to ensure that the children and young people in your school know what to do if they are concerned about a friend?

2. Aside from the strategies that Erin used, what other strategies could be employed by staff to help to keep Oonagh safe?

Helping someone grieving a suicide

In your role, you may be asked to support a child or young person who is grieving a loved one lost to suicide. This can be very emotionally demanding and put you at risk of experiencing some trauma yourself. This is why it is vitally important to access appropriate levels of supervision if you are asked to take on such a task. Chapter 15 focuses on the topic of supervision, and it is strongly recommended that any members of staff involved in supporting a child through a bereavement of this nature access regular supervision as an individual or within a small group.

When someone has lost a loved one to suicide, they may often feel isolated and stigmatized. When we try to help and support them, it is quite natural to feel awkward, but it is vital that we do not let this prevent us from giving our support. It is also important that we do not feel we have to provide all the answers or say all the right things. Most crucial is that we provide love, compassion and a listening ear. We also need to understand that the pain of suicide loss may lessen over time but will probably never totally pass.

Key dos and don'ts
Do:

- Acknowledge and accept that you may feel uncomfortable talking about suicide.

- Keep calm if you do not know what to say; just listening is more important. It is okay to admit that you do not know what to say. Nothing you can say will make the feelings go away, but the young person needs support and connection.

- Invite the young person to talk about the loved one and share memories, if they would like to. Allow them to express all of their emotions without judgement.

- Always use compassionate and appropriate language to talk about suicide.

Do not:

- Use the term 'committed suicide', as this implies that suicide is a criminal act and only serves to reinforce any stigma, making the grieving person feel more isolated (see 'Useful/helpful language' earlier in this chapter).

- Make judgements about the person who died, or label them as being 'weak' or 'selfish', as we know that suicide is the result of extreme emotional distress and not a character defect.

- Demand any explanation or make any speculation about the reasons why the person took their own life.

- Lose patience, as someone who has lost a loved one through suicide may need to talk at great length without being frightened of being judged or interrupted; remember that walking through the same points again and again can help the individual to come to terms with what happened.

Children and young people will have many questions when someone in their family dies. However, when a parent or close relative dies by suicide, these questions can seem much harder to answer. The problem is that when children don't have answers to these questions, they may devise their own explanations, and these can frequently be inaccurate and sometimes rather scary.

How you address the subject will generally depend on the child's age and ability to process the information given. However, it's important to remember that children very often understand much more than adults think they do. Many of these conversations are likely to happen between the child and their family; however, with the family's consent, their child may also be able to speak with you about what has happened. It is important to liaise closely with the family on this to ensure that there is a consistent approach.

Questions children might ask include:

- *'Why?'* – This is the most common question that both adults and children will ask when someone dies by suicide. It is important to remember that there is rarely a simple explanation and only the person who died can really know the answer to this question. Even when a parent who has died by suicide has left a note, the suicide can remain hard to understand. It is, therefore, important to keep your answers short and simple, using words that match the child's age and stage of development. It's also vital to provide information that the child wants, rather than overloading them with information you think they might need. It's usually the case that a child or young person will want to know more as time goes on so will then ask for more information.

  We can tell children that, when people die by suicide, it is usually because they are not well, and they are feeling unhappy. This unhappiness is not the kind of sadness that children might feel when they experience disappointment during their day, but rather a more serious kind of sadness that can go on for a considerable time.

  We can also tell children and young people that the parent was in a great deal of emotional pain and felt that living was just too hard for them. They did not believe that anyone could help them, and they also felt that they did not know how to get the kind of help they might need. They felt very sad and couldn't see another way to stop this sadness.

  When we are explaining suicide to younger children, it is important to use simple language. For example, 'Suicide is when a person is very sad and they end their life.'

- *'Is it my fault?'* – It is vital to reassure the child that suicide is never anyone's fault. You may need to repeat this message again and again.

  Children can often feel guilty when someone dies by suicide, worrying that they were somehow the cause of it. They may wonder if things could have been different had they done what they were told to do more often, or if they had not fought with their siblings, and so on. It is essential to be very clear with them that they did nothing wrong; the suicide was definitely not their fault and had nothing to do with anything they said or did in the past.

  It is also important to ensure that the child or young person understands that there was nothing that they could have done differently to prevent the parent's suicide. Alongside this, you need to make sure that the child or young person knows that the parent who died loved them very much.

  We know that feelings are not rational, and even when the child has been told that they are not to blame, they can still feel guilty, and these feelings can last for a long time. Providing children and young people the opportunity to express their guilt is essential, and eventually, these feelings will become less intense.

- *'Will I die by suicide as well? Are you going to die too?'* – Children and young people often find suicide very scary and can become concerned that they may end up dying in the same way. They may think it is genetic or 'runs in the family'. It is vital to assure them that you cannot catch suicide from someone else, like a cold, and it is certainly not inherited from one's parents.

- *'What will I tell my friends at school? Will they think I come from the "mad family"?'* – Lots of people have negative attitudes about suicide and mental health problems; some will stigmatize a family who have experienced a suicide, and those who have lost loved ones by suicide may find themselves being bullied in a school context. It is really important to help and support children at such times to practise statements that reflect the truth of the matter; for example, 'My mother was very sick and very, very sad.' It's also vital that children and young people are encouraged to report any such bullying at the outset.

  Supporting children in identifying just how much information to share with other children is also helpful. It is important that children understand that they have a choice about how much information they share; provide them with tools and strategies to stop conversations that they feel uncomfortable with, teaching them to use relevant scripts, such as, 'Thanks for asking, but I really don't want to talk about this at the moment.'

- *'Will I be this sad for ever?'* – Children and young people experience grief in different ways. However, their feelings about suicide can be different to those experienced after other kinds of death. Many can have quite extreme feelings of shame and embarrassment towards their parent who has died by suicide.

  It can be very difficult for children and young people to deal with such intense grief all of the time. They may, therefore, mourn in small chunks over a long period. They can cry one minute and then play with friends happily the next. This up-and-down part of the grieving process can be quite difficult for them to navigate, but also for adults who are trying to support them.

  It is important, therefore, to assure them that they will not always feel this way so that they can have a sense of hope. Encouraging them to talk about their feelings is vital; alternatively, they can explore such feelings through drawing and playing if they do not want to talk. Most important is that they feel heard and validated and that their feelings are normalized.

  Furthermore, children need to understand that this pain will reduce over time and that one of the best things that they can do is to talk about their loss, letting their feelings out – sometimes through crying, screaming or yelling, but also through asking questions. All of this is quite okay.

How can you help them to start feeling better?

Encourage them to ask questions and tell them not to be afraid of making themselves sadder by asking these questions and talking about the death of their loved one.

- Help them recognize that it is okay to feel happy and sad. Just because they are having a good day and enjoying something does not mean that they have forgotten their loved one.

- Use appropriate story books or literature to prompt the conversations. Make use of appropriate resources, such as a bereavement box, to support such conversations.

- Keep to normal routines as much as possible and encourage them to attend the usual after-school clubs or activities, as appropriate.

- Check out any relevant support groups that may be available to the child or young person, both in and out of the school context, and discuss whether or not these may be helpful to them.

- Ensure that the child has access to a relevant helpline so that they can discuss their thoughts and feelings with a professional, as and when they need to.

- Encourage the child or young person to keep a journal in order to process their feelings further.

- Ensure that fun times are actually scheduled into the child or young person's day.

- Check in with them often to ensure that the child or young person feels loved by those who are still there to nurture them.

- Encourage the child to use a range of tools and strategies to commemorate the person they have lost; for example, making up a special photo album or memory book.

- If the child talks about wanting to die, do take these comments seriously and immediately seek professional help. It is wrong to assume that the child or young person does not really mean it.

References

O'Connor, R. (2021) *When It Is Darkest: Why People Die by Suicide and What We Can Do to Prevent It*. Manchester: Vermilion.

Papyrus (2018) *Building Suicide-Safer Schools and Colleges: A Guide for Teachers and Staff*. https://papyrus-uk.org/wp-content/uploads/2018/10/400734-Schools-guide-PAPYRUS.pdf

Patalay, P. & Fitzsimons, E. (2020) *Mental Ill-health at Age 17 in the UK: Prevalence of and Inequalities in Psychological Distress, Self-Harm and Attempted Suicide*. London: Centre for Longitudinal Studies.

CHAPTER 14

Self-care

The importance of self-care

We know that dysregulated and stressed adults cannot effectively support and help children and young people who are also dysregulated and stressed. It is impossible.

We also know that the direct carers or nurturers of children are most effective in helping them develop self-regulation. They can provide activities that support regulation and are also the most immediate role models for children. The emotional tone of a school or home is dramatically affected by the capacity of adults to regulate themselves:

- If adults respond to children's distress or trauma in a *calm but engaged* way, they demonstrate an alternative way of managing stress.

- When adults respond to children's distress or trauma by becoming *dysregulated*, they replicate the damaging environments that characterized children's earlier or current experiences.

Van der Kolk (1994) describes trauma as 'speechless terror', and traumatized children may be slow to develop speech or may struggle to find words to describe their trauma or their feelings. Trauma and stress may also affect the capacity to process verbal information; traumatized children can struggle to follow complex directions and may experience auditory selectivity so that only part of a verbal communication is heard. As adults, we can often interpret failure to obey directions or respond to questions as wilful defiance and react punitively, rather than modifying our communication to match the child's needs.

So, once again, we need to be careful to ensure that our responses and the systems we put in place, both in the home and in school, ensure these factors are considered. We must respond appropriately to children and young people who have experienced trauma, stress and anxiety, and who have recently lived through the traumatic times of the COVID-19 pandemic. We need to create safety routines first and also change our own expectations and behaviours.

The prevalence of stress and anxiety disorders among children and young people is on the rise, meaning that we need to take a more pro-active approach towards developing essential skills for managing such issues, including relaxation and self-care strategies. This is the rationale for including a range of these strategies and techniques in this chapter. It is vital that school staff can and do model these to the children and young people they nurture.

To achieve this, we need to ensure that we know *how to engage in effective self-care and how to manage our own stress and anxiety*, while simultaneously *understanding the need to respond in a truly trauma-informed way*. In these difficult times, when we know that many children will be experiencing such a stressful social and educational context, this has never been more important.

> *'It took me a long time to realize that I needed to look after myself rather than always looking after the children and neglecting myself. I was always there but I wasn't really present. I was impatient and hassled.'* (Rachel, teaching assistant)

REFLECTION POINT

Think about your definition of self-care. What does this involve for you? What are you currently doing to manage your own levels of stress on a daily basis? What relaxation strategies are you using? How do you think that you model these to the children and young people you currently support?

These are all important questions to consider at the outset. Very often we think that we are looking after ourselves and then become surprised when we suddenly feel overwhelmed and stressed out. This is often because we are not keeping to a daily regime of self-care that is balanced and consistently used. Also, we sometimes fail to see what really does work and what doesn't work quite so well. Think about three things that you do now which really do work for you, and then try to think about three things that you might want to improve on.

Some important benefits of self-care include:

- *Increased productivity* – When you learn to set boundaries by saying 'no' to things that are too much for you and allowing time for what matters to you, you will be better able to focus on what is important. You will be able to work more efficiently and will bring creativity to your role that is so often stifled by stress.

- *Strengthened immune system* – Research suggests that many self-care activities, including deep breathing, mindfulness exercises and meditation, activate the part of the nervous system that combats stress and helps us to relax (De Couck et al., 2019; Gerritsen & Band, 2018). Stress, particularly over the long term, can have a negative impact on our physical health and immune system function. Therefore, better self-care means fewer illnesses, fewer days off sick and more time supporting the children that you work with.

- *Higher self-esteem* – Regularly making time to meet your own needs and put yourself first sends the message to your subconscious that you matter and that you are important. This can help to avoid cycles of negative thinking and increase your mood. We all know how contagious emotions can be, so the children in your care will benefit through your feeling calm and content.

- *Understanding yourself* – As children, we generally have a strong sense of what we love to do and what makes us happy. However, as adults, it is easy to lose touch with ourselves and forget what makes us happy. You may notice that you have spent so much time dedicated to children at school, and to your own family, that you have lost touch with yourself. Practising self-care means thinking about what you really love to do, leading to a better understanding of yourself and reigniting your passion for life.

- *Fills your bucket* – Self-care gives you the energy and headspace needed to be compassionate to others. Being compassionate and kind can be thought of as like filling a bucket; you can't fill someone else's bucket if your own is empty.

Is self-care selfish?

The answer is NO!

A big problem for many of us is that self-care sometimes feels self-indulgent, or in some way selfish. This is despite the fact that, as is often said, we need to put on our own oxygen mask before we try to help someone else.

Self-care involves recognizing your flaws and being compassionate to yourself in identifying your own needs. It also often means making compromises and recognizing that you cannot do everything for everyone. For instance, you might be torn between being at home with loved ones and time at work. You may feel guilty about spending time doing something for yourself rather than being with your family. Self-compassion involves coping the best that you can, without criticizing or punishing yourself for not meeting unattainable ideals of perfection. Self-care also involves being able to say 'no' when your wellbeing is being compromised.

Being the role model

Being able to develop skills of positive thinking is essential if we are to model self-care behaviours and attitudes to the children and young people we care for. Here are some ways to make positive changes to your thoughts and behaviours:

- To become a more optimistic and positive person, you need to identify the areas of your life where you usually think negatively. This could be work-related, your daily commute or even your relationships. Start by focusing on one area and try to approach it in a more positive way.

- It is important to reflect upon your thinking frequently during the day. If you notice that your thoughts are mainly negative, try to spin them positively.

- Humour can be a great stress reliever. So, allow yourself to smile or laugh, especially during difficult times. Seek humour in everyday situations and events.

- Follow a healthy lifestyle by aiming to exercise for about 30 minutes most days of the week. You can even break this up into shorter chunks of time during the day. Exercise can positively affect your mood and reduce stress.

- Surround yourself with supportive people who make you feel good. Negative people may increase your stress levels and make it difficult for you to manage stress in healthy ways.

- Practise positive self-talk by following a simple rule: do not say anything to yourself that you wouldn't say to anyone else. Be kind and supportive in your self-talk. When confronted with negative thoughts, assess them rationally and counteract them with affirmations highlighting your positive qualities. Reflect on aspects of your life that you are grateful for.

CASE STUDY

Margaret works full-time as a teaching assistant in a large primary school. Her husband has a chronic illness, meaning that he is unable to work, and Margaret has three teenage children. Margaret spends a lot of time supporting children with their social skills and emotional regulation. Margaret has excellent relationships with the children, and, while she acknowledges that she loves to feel needed by them, it is also placing a huge pressure on her shoulders. Margaret's husband also relies on her, and her own children are struggling with their wellbeing since the pandemic. Margaret feels torn in too many directions and can't help feeling that she is letting them all down. Margaret hardly ever takes a day off as she is worried about how the children at school will cope without her. So many of them see her as their 'safe person'. However, Margaret is feeling increasingly exhausted. She holds it together at school and then loses her patience easily with her family when she gets home.

Recently, Margaret realized that she could not be the person that they all need her to be without also looking after herself. It took Margaret a while to remember what she enjoyed doing because it had been so long since she had thought about herself and her needs. Margaret has made the decision to start walking home from work instead of driving. While this means that she isn't able to get home so quickly to her family, she loves being outdoors, getting some exercise, and having a bit of time alone with her thoughts. When she arrives home every evening, she feels refreshed and has more energy. She finds that it gives her time to process what has happened during the day, so that she can leave her thoughts and worries at the door rather than bringing them home with her. This tiny change, of 20 minutes to herself each day, has made a huge difference to Margaret, both in school and at home. She is now more patient, compassionate and able to contain the emotions of others.

Questions

1. What do you do for you?

2. What really makes your heart sing?

3. Do you feel that you are meeting your own needs?

4. What small change could you make for yourself today?

Top tips and strategies

There are *five main categories of self-care* for us all to consider and attempt to fit into our daily routines and activities:

- Sensory

- Emotional

- Spiritual

- Physical

- Social

Sensory self-care

Sensory self-care is about calming your mind. We need to be able to sense what is happening around us, allowing us to live in the present moment. Living in the present moment lessens our stress as our anxiety tends to relate to events that have happened in the past, or things that may occur in our future. Purposefully focusing on the present moment allows us freedom from those concerns. Sensory self-care, also often referred to as mindfulness, refers to focusing on our senses (taste, smell, touch, sound and sight).

Some suggestions for sensory self-care:

- listening to the sound of an open fire

- snuggling up under a warm, soft blanket

- going for a nature walk and focusing on the smell of the air

- stroking a pet

- having a massage or taking time to massage your hands with hand cream

- noticing the feeling of the bubbles popping against your skin in the bath

- focusing on your breathing and how your body feels as it relaxes

- lying down and listening to your favourite music with your eyes closed

- sitting outside and noticing the details in what you can see around you

- eating chocolate slowly, really savouring how it tastes and feels in your mouth

- walking barefoot in sand, feeling it between your toes.

Emotional self-care

Rather than suppressing, ignoring or distracting yourself from your emotions, allow yourself to really feel them and accept them, so that you can let them go. Remember that all our emotions are there for a reason, and no emotions are good or bad. It is natural and normal to feel angry, worried or upset sometimes. We only need to hold ourselves accountable for how we behave in response to our emotions.

Some suggestions for emotional self-care:

- keeping a journal of your emotions

- making a list of 'feelings words' to expand your emotional vocabulary – being able to label an emotion accurately helps to reduce the intensity with which it is felt

- allowing yourself a good cry if you need to; this can help to pro-vide a sense of release and completes the stress cycle, allowing you to return to a balanced, soothed emotional state

- talking to a friend or family member who makes time to listen to you and understand your feelings

- thinking about and visualizing times when you have felt at your happiest

- listening to songs that resonate with how you feel.

Spiritual self-care

Spiritual self-care is not necessarily about following a particular faith or believing in God. It is more about having a sense of meaning and purpose. This is a key component to wellbeing and features heavily in the research regarding happiness and flourishing.

REFLECTION POINT

– What is your reason for being?

– Why do you do your job?

Some suggestions for spiritual self-care:

- practising meditation or mindfulness every day, through formal practice (e.g. 10-minute meditation), or informal practice (e.g. mindfully cleaning your teeth)

- attending a religious service if you follow a faith

- reading poetry

- going for a walk in the countryside and noticing all of the beauty around you

- making a list at the start of each day of three things that you are grateful for

- releasing your creativity, perhaps through painting, craft, making music or writing

- making a concerted effort to notice the things that make you feel most alive, and thinking about how you can make more time for these in your life

- making a photo album of all the things and people that make you feel the happiest.

Physical self-care

Our physical health is of paramount importance when it comes to self-care. Exercise is important for our physical health and wellbeing, but also for our mental wellbeing, by helping us to use up the energy that may have been released when feeling under stress and by producing endorphins. This is our body's natural way of numbing pain, helping us to feel calm and increasing our mood.

REFLECTION POINT

- Do you do regular physical activity?

- If not, what is one small step that you could take towards improving this?

Some suggestions for physical self-care:

- going for a walk during your lunch break

- playing a game with the children at break time

- walking or cycling to and from work

- doing an online exercise routine before/after work

- having a step target each day

- suggesting having a weekly exercise class for staff after school (e.g. yoga/ dance/Zumba, etc.)

- joining a running group or local sports club

- eating healthily

- giving yourself the opportunity to get seven to nine hours' sleep each night.

Social self-care

During the pandemic, we saw more than ever the importance of connecting with others for our mental health and wellbeing. Relationships are key to being able to respond to adversity with resilience. Many of us have a need to make regular opportunities to see our friends and family, as this boosts our happiness. However, it is important to consider how the presence of others makes you feel. Make time for those that make you feel good and allow yourself to set boundaries with those who don't. This also depends on our personality type. Those who are more introverted may also need to make time for themselves, away from other people, particularly if socializing is anxiety-provoking.

REFLECTION POINT

– Do you consider yourself an introvert or an extrovert?

– Who are the people that bring out the best in you, and make you feel happiest? How can you ensure that you make time to see them?

– Are there people in your life that have a negative impact on your wellbeing? What boundaries can you set to protect your wellbeing?

'I had a friend from school and our friendship carried on because we had known each other for so long. I would get a sinking feeling every time that she messaged me and dread having to meet up. She would just make snide remarks and didn't seem to really care how I was or what I had been up to. I kept seeing her because I didn't want to upset her or seem unkind, but I would always come home feeling upset and angry. I spoke to another friend about how I was feeling, and I realized that it was okay to put myself first. I started to say 'no' more to things that didn't make me feel good and it's really helped.' (*Laura, teacher*)

Some suggestions for social self-care:

- making a date to meet up with a good friend

- sending a message to someone to tell them that you miss them or are thinking of them

- joining a group of people who share your interests (e.g. a choir, sports club, PTA, etc.)

- stopping socializing with those who undermine or disempower you – if you can't avoid them completely, setting boundaries to protect your wellbeing

- joining a support group for people who may struggle with the same things you do

- enrolling for a class to learn something new and meet new people.

REFLECTION POINT

This chapter is intended to be very practical and user-friendly, providing you with some helpful tools and strategies to develop and maintain an effective self-care regime.

It would be helpful at this point to take some time to reflect on the kinds of skills you might need to develop further, and how making use of this publication might help you to do exactly that. Undertaking a SWOT analysis is one way to identify: your current strengths, both within yourself and in your home or workplace; any weaknesses, or areas you may feel you need additional support with at this time; any opportunities to develop your skills and knowledge; and any threats that might impact negatively on your role, performance and, in particular, your ability to foster the post-traumatic growth of our vulnerable children and young people.

A photocopiable sheet for completing a SWOT analysis is provided on the next page. Once you have completed this analysis, you will probably have a greater understanding as to what support you may need going forward to effectively undertake your role and maintain your own wellbeing via a good self-care regime.

SWOT ANALYSIS: SELF-CARE	
Strengths	**Weaknesses**
The strengths that you have in looking after your own wellbeing:	Your areas for improvement in looking after your own wellbeing:
How does your school support your wellbeing and encourage self-care?	Areas for development within the school for supporting staff wellbeing and self-care:
Opportunities	**Threats**
Opportunities to look after your own wellbeing and make time for yourself:	Risks in making more time for yourself (consider also how they could be overcome):
Opportunities for your school to facilitate staff in looking after their wellbeing (e.g. reducing workload):	What risks are there for schools in supporting the self-care of staff?

References

De Couck, M., Caers, R., Musch, L., Fliegauf, J., Giangreco, A. & Gidron, Y. (2019) 'How breathing can help you make better decisions: Two studies on the effects of breathing patterns on heart rate variability and decision-making in business cases.' *International Journal of Psychophysiology, 139*, 1–9. doi:10.1016/j.ijpsycho.2019.02.011

Gerritsen, R.J.S. & Band, G.P.H. (2018) 'Breath of life: The respiratory vagal stimulation model of contemplative activity.' *Frontiers in Human Neuroscience, 12*. doi:10.3389/fnhum.2018.00397

Van der Kolk, B.A. (1994) 'The body keeps the score: Memory and the evolving psycho-biology of post-traumatic stress.' *Harvard Review of Psychiatry, 1*, 253–265.

CHAPTER 15

Supervision and Peer Support

A key element of being able to work successfully in supporting children and young people with their mental health is accessing appropriate support from colleagues. Historically, there has been a shortage of such support in education, particularly in terms of proper clinical supervision for staff in schools. However, when you are in a role that involves working therapeutically with children and young people, it is *essential that you access appropriate supervision* from someone who really understands your role, can help you process your own feelings and experiences, and can ensure that you support young people in an ethical and safe manner.

Supervision is a widely accepted norm in the fields of counselling, psychotherapy and other mental health disciplines. It is also a common practice in various professions that deal with both children and adults.

The process involves having regular meetings with another professional who possesses training in supervision skills. The meetings are structured and are designed to discuss casework and other professional issues. Supervision can be done on a one-to-one basis or in a group. Sometimes, there is a supervisor and supervisee relationship, but also supervision can be provided for each other within the same meeting (peer supervision). The primary purpose of supervision is to assist the practitioner in reflecting on and learning from their experiences. Milne (2007) defines clinical supervision as:

> The formal provision, by approved supervisors, of a relationship-based education and training that is work-focused and which manages, supports, develops and evaluates the work of colleague/s. The main methods that supervisors use are corrective feedback on the supervisee's

performance, teaching, and collaborative goal-setting. It therefore differs from related activities, such as mentoring and coaching, by incorporating an evaluative component. Supervision's objectives are 'normative' (e.g. quality control), 'restorative' (e.g. encourage emotional processing) and 'formative' (e.g. maintaining and facilitating supervisees' competence, capability and general effectiveness).

Professionals such as chaplains, psychologists, mental health practitioners, counsellors, occupational therapists and art, music and drama therapists have been using supervision in their practice for a long time. In other disciplines – specifically in education – the practice may not be as evident or so well developed. The exception to this within education are emotional literacy support assistants (ELSAs), who receive half-termly group supervision with an educational psychologist.

REFLECTION POINT

What is your understanding of supervision right now? Do you have any experience of being supported in delivering your role? What kind of support do you currently access? Does this support help you to deliver support for children and young people you nurture? Does this support also help you to manage the emotional labour of your role? Is your line manager able to provide you with both performance management and wellbeing management?

It is important to reflect on these questions at the outset. The role of supporting young people with mental health issues is demanding and can be emotionally challenging. This is why, throughout this publication, we have reinforced the need for you to access appropriate professional and personal support.

If you are concerned that the support currently on offer is not adequate, do please identify who you can talk to in the school context to discuss this in more depth and to work together to try and find a solution.

Management supervision
Moving from performance management
to a focus on wellbeing

So, what would we expect managers to be looking for when supporting your wellbeing and ensuring that you are fit for purpose in delivering interventions and supporting children on a daily basis? You may find it helpful to share this section with your line manager, so that these points can be considered during your supervision sessions.

When looking at supporting your wellbeing, managers need to consider the areas of wellbeing discussed in Chapter 1 – spiritual, emotional, physical and mental wellbeing (see Figure 1.1). You may like to suggest that your line managers focus on some of the following questions before looking at performance:

- How do you feel currently, in terms of your wellbeing?

- How have you been managing your time and balancing priorities lately?

- Is your work–life balance working for you, or do you need to make any adjustments?

- Do you have enough time to reflect and give purpose to what you're doing inside and outside of work?

- What changes do you think you could make to support your own wellbeing?

- Can you think of any changes you could make now or in the future?

- What can I do as your line manager to support you with this?

In the past, educational contexts have not been particularly focused on supervision support for their staff, and have generally made use of performance management, which focuses on output and target-setting and professional development, as opposed to staff wellbeing and their ability to manage the emotional labour and processing necessary to do the job well. This is *particularly pertinent for staff who support some of our most vulnerable children and young people* in their role.

From our perspective, the supervision process is interactive: that is, a two-way communication based on trust. This communication may involve the following: solution-focused dialogue leading to well-formed outcomes; active listening; pacing and leading; framing and reframing;

problem analysis; non-judgemental challenge; positive by-products; association/disassociation; and future pacing.

The idea here is to facilitate thinking rather than to be directive; that is, the supervisor acts as a co-constructor in negotiating solutions and a way forward. Figure 15.2 illustrates this process in the four key areas of setting agenda, identifying the purpose, clarifying the processes involved, and outlining the potential outcomes of the supervision process.

CASE STUDY

Harsha had been involved in supporting a 14-year-old who was struggling with emotionally based school avoidance (EBSA). Harsha felt that she was carrying a lot of pressure on her shoulders to support the young person, who was extremely distressed, and also to help them to make progress. This role meant that Harsha sometimes did home visits, and her plans often had to change very quickly depending on how the young person was feeling that day, so that she could be there to meet them at the gate and support them in separating from their parent. Witnessing this high level of anxiety and distress, day in and day out, was taking its toll on Harsha. She was feeling under a lot of pressure from the senior leadership team, who were frustrated by the slow progress and wanted Harsha to take a 'tough love' approach.

Harsha had made a good relationship with the young person and their parents, and they were working together well, but Harsha was doubting herself and felt very alone. The mental health lead had been supportive of Harsha and arranged for her to meet with the educational psychologist (EP) for some supervision. The EP encouraged Harsha to reflect on the progress that had been made, and asked questions rather than giving advice. This allowed Harsha to explore alternative ideas and ways of thinking, and by the end she felt reassured and empowered, and the pressure on her shoulders had somehow been completely lifted.

Questions

1. Have you ever felt alone with a difficult situation, like Harsha?
2. Who did you talk to then?
3. Who could you talk to in the future?

AGENDAS/ISSUES

- Individual children/young people to discuss
- Staff team
- Specialist knowledge
- Personal issues and emotional aspects

- Practice experiences (e.g. ethical, moral, organizational, assessment/communication issues)
- Achievements

PUPOSE OF SUPERVISION

- Emotional support
- Affirmation
- Opportunity to reflect
- Integration and evaluation of experiences and practice, in terms of professional judgement, moral and ethical standards, personal belief systems and attitudes

- Identification of strategies and problem-solving
- Planning and target setting
- Knowledge and skills sharing and development

PROCESS

- Building rapport
- Co-construction of agenda
- Sharing of experience and knowledge
- Interactive communication
- Solution-focused dialogue
- Active listening

- Pacing and leading
- Framing and reframing
- Non-judgemental challenge
- Facilitation of thinking rather than being directive
- Presentation of other perspectives

OUTCOMES

- Changed state, e.g. reduction in stress, feeling valued
- New understanding(s) and perspectives(s)
- New knowledge

- Increased feelings of confidence and competence
- Strategy and resource generation
- Sense of belonging, empathy and support

FIGURE 15.2 SUPERVISION PROCESS

Peer supervision

It may be possible for you to also access support from a group of peers who are engaging in similar work in supporting children and young people with their wellbeing and mental health. This may take the form of peer supervision groups, which are becoming increasingly common in education. This can be very helpful in complementing any individual supervision and support, while also reinforcing that your peer group is possibly one of the most significant sources of support you will ever identify in the school context. People will have done work similar to you, gone through similar experiences, had similar questions; perhaps they will have found solutions and be able to share their knowledge base and skills. Never underestimate the power of the group and the power of peer support.

So, what is peer supervision?

Peer supervision differs from other more traditional forms of supervision, as it doesn't require the presence of a more qualified, identified 'expert' (e.g. a mental health lead, educational psychologist, etc.). Instead, peer supervision involves a group of colleagues all supporting each other in the supervision process for mutual benefit. The advantage of this is having a readily available group of peers who all understand your role and context. It does not rely on the availability of educational psychologists, who are in short supply across the UK, and means that you can more easily access supervision exactly when it is needed. Sometimes, these groups are all from one school, or they can be from across multiple schools.

You may find it useful to set up groups of people who are all in the same role (e.g. teachers), or multidisciplinary groups, with teaching assistants, teachers, senior leadership and so on, all within one group, sharing from each other's different experiences. The idea of these groups is to be supportive in allowing staff to reflect on situations and student needs, as well as their own needs. Groups may help each other in coming to a shared understanding and support each other in identifying their own solutions. The process should be empowering, solution-focused and helpful to everyone to feel part of a team in which all are invested in supporting the young person and each other. This process supports the development of empathy and should reduce stress for all involved. It provides much-needed breathing space to explore your own feelings about a situation, which so often go unconsidered. In some schools, this process is facilitated by an educational psychologist in the first instance and until schools feel confident running these sessions independently.

What could possibly go wrong?

Peer supervision groups need to be carefully managed to ensure that they remain effective, respectful and supportive. If you don't finish the session feeling empowered and replenished, these are some things that may have gone wrong:

- If there is no clear agenda or structure for discussions, sessions can descend into gossiping, griping or just chatting without direction.

- Inconsistent attendance can mean that sessions are not prioritized, and members no longer feel safe and supported. Building rapport as a group is impossible if membership is constantly changing.

- Group members may worry about being judged and therefore not feel safe sharing their practice.

- There could have been too much advice-giving without having empathized first. Solutions can be offered, but, ultimately, it's important to leave the power in the hands of the person who presented the problem.

- The clinical skills within the group may not be sufficient to handle the issues raised.

- Some group members may dominate, leaving others feeling frustrated or intimidated.

- People could be feeling criticized or demoralized.

'Our peer supervision group is wonderful. It definitely feels like a safe space where I can really share my thoughts without feeling judged. I feel really supported, never patronized, the ideas shared are great, and I always leave feeling reinvigorated.' (Patricia, emotional literacy support assistant)

'There is one person in our group who tends to dominate. He is very

negative about everything, and it can be quite draining. He also gives out advice in a way that makes me feel stupid. I don't feel that I get much from the sessions, to be honest, which is a shame.' (Heather, teaching assistant)

REFLECTION POINT

Consider times when you have felt very supported by members of your peer group. What was the context? What did you need from them, and what did you receive? How was it helpful, and how could it have been more helpful to you? Think about whether or not accessing regular peer group support sessions might be something useful for developing you both professionally and personally in your role.

Top tips and strategies
Setting the right atmosphere

There are four key components in setting up a successful peer supervision group, and these should be emphasized at the outset to ensure that all participants are aware of their importance:

- *Trust* –Participants who trust each other will speak more openly.

- *Confidentiality* – Information should remain confidential within the group.

- *Support* – Participants should always try to support each other.

- *Respect* – Mutual appreciation promotes openness.

For supervision to be effective, it is important to create an atmosphere in which group members feel able to talk openly about issues, reflect on their weaknesses and acknowledge difficulties. The group should be without any hierarchy or personal conflict, and mutual trust is key.

Format for supervision session

There are a variety of ways to structure a supervision session, but a framework of some sort is necessary to keep it feeling supportive and to maintain focus on the issues at hand. At the outset, you will need one person to chair the meeting. Their role is to set the agenda, keep everyone on task and manage the time to ensure that all agenda items are covered within the allocated time. The chair may change during each session; this is advisable to ensure that a hierarchy does not emerge within the group. You will also need to assign someone the role of time-keeper, and that person will need access to a stopwatch. It is their role to time each section of the supervision process and signal to the group when it is time to move on to the next part.

Setting the agenda

When setting the agenda, the chair should ask each person whether they have something that they would like to discuss in the meeting. Common items on the agenda in peer supervision might be an issue with a child or young person that they would like to discuss, a resource or source of information that they have found helpful, or sharing a success story or something that has gone well since the last supervision session. Once you have the list of items for the agenda, it is helpful to assign timings to each item on the list to help manage the time. Using the problem-solving framework described below, issues will generally need 20 minutes, while sharing a resource or success story would only require about five minutes. Allocating time will allow you to ensure that all agenda items are covered within the timeframe, or to prioritize agenda items from the outset if there are too many issues to cover during one supervision session.

Problem-solving

Where members of the group come to supervision with a specific issue that they would like to discuss, the following steps are useful in ensuring that the focus remains on their issue, the responses that they receive are supportive, and they end the session feeling empowered. The timer will need to signal when it is time to move on to the next step, and the chair should explain what is to happen during each stage of the framework.

- *Step 1: Describing the problem* (4 minutes) – The problem-owner should be given four minutes to describe the issue in as much detail as they can without being interrupted. If they stop before the time finishes, encourage them to continue by asking, 'Is there anything else that might be useful for us to know?' Often, this will jumpstart the person back into giving more detail, and they may still be in full flow when the timer goes after four minutes.

- *Step 2: Asking questions* (4 minutes) – The rest of the group can now ask information-gathering questions to find out more pertinent information. The group should be careful to avoid giving advice or straying into finding solutions at this point, just focusing on questions that will allow the problem-owner to explore the issue further.

- *Step 3: Goldfish bowl technique* (4 minutes) – At this point, the problem-owner can sit back, while the rest of the group reflect together about what they have heard. They should not address the problem-owner and should pretend that they are not there. The problem-owner may like to take a seat out of the circle to create that boundary, while ensuring that they can still see and hear everything that is happening with the group. The rest of the group may reflect on the issue itself, and what might be going on beneath the surface, or the group may also reflect on the emotions that they can sense in the problem-owner in relation to the issue. Try to focus on the thoughts, feelings and behaviours of all involved to try to make some sense of what you have heard. Some discussions may prompt more questions, in which case you may like to wonder aloud about some further questions that you have. The purpose of this activity is to allow the person to step away and put distance between themselves and the problem, so that they can see with more clarity and take a more objective stance.

- *Step 4: Solution-finding* (6 minutes) – The problem-owner should now be invited back into the circle. They should spend the first few minutes reflecting on the group's discussions and putting forward solutions or possible ways forward that have come to mind during those discussions. Following this, the group should be invited to pose possible next steps or solutions to the issue. The group needs to ensure that these solutions are provided in a respectful way that does not disempower or belittle the problem-owner.

- *Step 5: The way forward* (2 minutes) – The solution must always lie in the hands, and remain in possession, of the problem-owner. They have the final word on deciding what their next steps will be from the suggestions given by the group.

Essential factors for effective peer group supervision

1. No hierarchy

The term 'peer' refers to all members of the group being of equal status. In a peer supervision group, no one should have significantly more or less status than any other by way of seniority or experience. If one member is accountable to another in the group (their line manager or head of department), that will limit the effectiveness of the supervision. Everyone in the group needs to feel able to speak about their practice without fear of judgement or consequence.

2. Supportive ethos

A supportive ethos within the group is essential for group members to feel safe and supervision to be successful. There needs to be an implicit assumption that 'people do the best they can with the resources they have' and 'it's okay to make mistakes'. This will allow group members to feel able to share safely and honestly, without judgement or feeling inadequate. The need to be seen as competent in front of others will limit the effectiveness of the supervision, as we have to allow ourselves to be vulnerable to learn from our mistakes or take guidance from others. Therefore, a non-competitive environment needs to be created, free from judgement and consequence, in which all have the freedom to be honest.

3. Structure

The approach to peer supervision described above is highly structured, and the importance of a framework has been detailed. The structure provides the leadership that an appointed supervisor would usually bring. It also creates safety and helps the group to maintain appropriate boundaries and avoid common pitfalls.

4. Showing up

The group need to place importance on supervision, and respect one another by prioritizing attendance. This gives the group the message that they are valued, important and supported, and also helps to keep the group membership consistent. When groups are made up of members who rarely attend, it can alter the rapport and dynamic within the group when they do show up, making it feel less safe to share.

5. Confidentiality

This is an essential ground rule for successful peer supervision groups. It means that when the full stop is placed at the end of an individual's supervision time, there is no further discussion of the issue beyond the confines of the group. This contributes to the safety that is essential for individuals to fully engage in this self-directed process. The exception to this would be when there is a safeguarding concern, and you feel that the information needs to be shared to keep the person, or those around them, safe. In most cases, you should sensitively explain who you will be passing the information on to and what will happen. There may be other situations where you feel that speaking to someone outside of the peer supervision group about an issue would be helpful, but this should only be done with the person's explicit consent and in partnership with them.

It is helpful to keep a record of supervision so that you have notes of the actions that come from it, as well as other reflection points, and can prepare for the next session. A downloadable template for keeping a record of supervision is provided in the Appendices.

Reference

Milne, D.,(2007) 'An empirical definition of clinical supervision.' *British Journal of Clinical Psychology, 46*(4), 437–447, doi:10.1348/014466507x197415

Where to Get More Help

If you would like more information on any of the areas covered in this handbook, here are some websites, books and resources that you may find helpful, all of which are available and correct at the point of going to press.

Understanding mental health

Charlie Waller Trust https://charliewaller.org

> Charitable organization offering evidence-based resources, information and training for school staff, parents and young people.

Young Minds www.youngminds.org.uk

> Young Minds offer a wealth of resources and information for young people, educators and parents on a wide range of mental health issues. Their young person-friendly website offers guidance and support, as well as timely data from their own research into the mental health needs of young people.

Bounce Together www.bouncetogether.co.uk

> Bounce Together provide an online survey platform to allow schools to measure and monitor the wellbeing and mental health of staff and pupils. It has many standardized wellbeing surveys ready to be sent out at the touch of a button, meaning that administering and analysing wellbeing data can be quick, easy and monitored closely.

Mentally Healthy Schools www.mentallyhealthyschools.org.uk

Mentally Healthy Schools have resources and information on a range of mental health issues. Subscribe to their mailing list to receive regular mental health toolkits to use with children and young people.

Anna Freud Centre – Schools in Mind www.annafreud.org/schools-and-colleges

Schools in Mind provide resources, training and the '5 Steps' framework to support schools in developing a whole-school approach to mental health.

Education Support www.educationsupport.org.uk

Emotional support and resources for the staff working in education.

Reflective practice

CPD Coffee Time with Dr Tina Rae: 12. Reflective Practice www.youtube.com/watch?v=3Mpf_r-J8pA

A free webinar covering this theme in detail.

Cambridge Assessment International Education www.cambridge-community.org.uk/professional-development/gswrp/index.html

This post extends the learning about reflective practice, referring to the models by Kolb and Gibb.

Trauma Informed Schools UK https://traumainformedschools.co.uk/what-is-a-trauma-informed-school

This organization provides resources and training on incorporating a trauma-informed approach. Of particular relevance are their links to the importance of having an emotionally available adult, or 'Always Available Adult' (AAA).

University of Cambridge https://libguides.cam.ac.uk/reflectivepractice toolkit/introduction

This 'Reflective Practice Toolkit' contains scripts and frameworks to help support the development of reflective practice, particularly for those who are new to the concept.

Active listening

Client-centred Therapy: Its Current Practice, Implications and Theory **(by Carl Rogers)**

The original, comprehensive guide to active listening. This is an in-depth but easy read for those who really want to learn more about active listening and counselling skills. A new edition was published in 2003.

Active Listening **(by Rogers & Farson)**

This short pocketbook is a useful go-to guide to some of the techniques of active listening for those who want something more concise.

Attachment needs and developmental trauma

Attachment in the Classroom **(by Heather Geddes)**

Classic text for understanding the basics of attachment theory and how it relates to classroom practice. It includes lots of case studies to illustrate the theory, as well as practical recommendations.

Inside I'm Hurting **(by Louise Bomber)**

Along with her other books, this book contains lots of useful advice for supporting children who have experienced developmental trauma. A must-read for this topic.

Creating Trauma-Informed, Strengths-Based Classrooms: Teacher Strategies for Nurturing Students' Healing, Growth, and Learning **(by Brunzell & Norrish)**

This book is informative but easily accessible and applies research based on attachment theory and trauma-informed practice, and research from the area of positive psychology, to the classroom environment.

Adverse Childhood Experiences (ACEs) Early Trauma Online Learning
www.acesonlinelearning.com

Free online training on understanding attachment, adverse childhood experiences and trauma-informed practice. Perfect for school staff who want to develop their understanding of the impact of trauma on the brain and behaviour.

Beacon House https://beaconhouse.org.uk

Beacon House is a therapeutic service for young people, families and adults who have experienced trauma and loss. Their website has lots of free resources.

Emotion coaching
Raising an Emotionally Intelligent Child (by Gottman and DeClaire)

This is the key text for introducing emotion coaching. Although it is aimed at parents, it is all highly applicable to school staff in their practice with children and young people.

Emotion Coaching UK www.emotioncoachinguk.com

Founded by psychologist Licette Gus, this website has lots of resources, as well as access to training for school staff.

Anxiety
The Happiness Trap: Evolution of the Human Mind www.youtube.com/watch?v=kv6HkipQcfA

Russ Harris, one of the most prominent authors in the field of acceptance and commitment therapy (ACT), developed a series of animations that beautifully explain anxiety and how it has evolved. Another episode of the series, called 'The Struggle Switch', is also a very helpful concept for lots of young people who are struggling to cope with anxiety.

The Anxious Child www.mentalhealth.org.uk/sites/default/files/anxious_child.pdf

A freely available booklet for parents and carers to learn more about supporting their child with anxiety.

BBC Bitesize Parents Toolkit www.bbc.co.uk/bitesize/articles/zfnhxbk?utm_source=google&utm_medium=cpc&utm_campaign=anxiety

BBC Bitesize have provided a number of short videos for parents and carers in supporting anxiety. These 'bitesize' videos are also helpful for busy school staff who need to find information and support quickly and easily.

Starving the Anxiety Gremlin: A Cognitive Behavioural Therapy Workbook on Anxiety Management **(by Kate Collins-Donnelly)**

There are two workbooks, one for ages 5–9, and one for ages 10+. They contain lots of information that is useful for school staff but presented in a way that is accessible to children and young people. There are also lots of activities and strategies to try.

Self-harm
Calm Harm https://calmharm.co.uk

Calm Harm is an app based on dialectical behaviour therapy (DBT), which helps young people to meet their emotional needs (comfort, release, etc.) without harming themselves. The app provides some activities and techniques to help young people to break the cycle of self-harm and explore underlying triggers.

Charlie Waller Foundation https://charliewaller.org/resources/young-people-who-self-harm

The Charlie Waller Foundation have produced two guides, one for school staff and one for parents, full of information and evidence-based guidance for supporting young people who self-harm.

Mentally Healthy Schools www.mentallyhealthyschools.org.uk/mental-health-needs/self-harm/what-schools-and-further-education-settings-can-do

> This webpage has advice for primary and secondary schools in supporting children who may be self-harming. It also provides a useful guide on approaching difficult conversations about mental health with young people.

Understanding and Preventing Self-Harm in Schools: Effective Strategies for Identifying Risk and Providing Support (by Tina Rae and Jody Walshe)

> A book that provides an abundance of advice and support to tackle this difficult issue safely and with confidence.

Alumina www.selfharm.co.uk

> Alumina is a free online course, run by counsellors and youth workers, for 11- to 19-year-olds, to help reduce self-harm behaviours and support them in coping with their emotions.

Panic attacks

Clear Fear app www.clearfear.co.uk

> This app uses a cognitive behavioural approach to support young people in understanding and managing anxiety and panic attacks.

Childline www.childline.org.uk/info-advice/your-feelings/anxiety-stress-panic/coping-panic-attacks

> Useful information that is easily accessible for children and young people experiencing panic attacks, but also helpful for adults who are supporting them, with tips on helping someone who is experiencing a panic attack.

Anxiety Canada www.anxietycanada.com/articles/home-management-strategies-for-panic-disorder

> Strategies for parents to use at home to support their child to understand and manage panic attacks.

TED-ED animation (by Cindy J. Aaronson, directed by Aim Creative Studios) www.youtube.com/watch?v=IzFObkVRSVo

> A short animation detailing the science behind panic attacks, what they are and how they can be prevented.

Supporting Adolescents with Stress and Anxiety **(by Tina Rae, Jody Walshe & Jo Wood)**

> A practical, accessible guide with lots of resources and ideas to use with adolescents.

Depression

Kooth www.kooth.com

> Free, confidential service offering online support for young people. Support includes information, resources, discussion groups, webchat, a daily journal and crisis support.

Campaign Against Living Miserably www.thecalmzone.net

> CALM is a charitable organization specifically aimed at raising awareness of men's mental health and preventing suicides in young men. They have a huge amount of information and guidance on their website, including inspirational stories from male role models in the public eye, speaking about their mental health struggles.

Catch It app

> Catch It has been developed by researchers at the University of Liverpool and uses tools from cognitive behavioural therapy (CBT) to help young people to recognize their unhelpful thoughts and challenge them.

Grief, loss and bereavement

Grief Encounter www.griefencounter.org.uk

> A charitable organization supporting children and young people who have experienced a bereavement. They provide resources, advice and counselling for children of all ages and those who support them.

The Bereavement Box (by Tina Rae)

A box containing cards with many different thought-provoking, reassuring and comforting activities for children and young people who have experienced a bereavement.

The Bereavement Book (by Tina Rae)

Practical activities to support young people of all ages through bereavement and grief.

Winston's Wish www.winstonswish.org

A charitable organization set up with the aim of giving hope to grieving children. They have produced many resources and publications, and their website is a treasure trove of useful information and advice for those supporting a child or young person going through a bereavement.

Child Bereavement UK www.childbereavementuk.org

Child Bereavement UK supports children and their families following a bereavement. They also have many resources and training courses for school staff, including for complex situations in which there has been a particularly traumatic death.

Eating disorders

BEAT Eating Disorders www.beateatingdisorders.org.uk

The charity provides guidance and help to those suffering with an eating disorder, as well as those who are supporting someone with an eating disorder.

Promoting Positive Body Image in Teenagers (by Tina Rae and Ali D'Amario)

A 10-session evidence-based intervention programme supporting teenagers in developing media literacy skills, self-esteem and respecting their bodies for what they can do rather than how they look.

Banish Your Body Image Thief (by Kate Collins-Donnelly)

A self-help book for young people, using a cognitive behavioural approach to help them challenge their negative thinking about themselves and their bodies.

Self-Harm and Eating Disorders in Schools (by Pooky Knightsmith)

Lots of useful research-based information and advice for those working in schools. Crucially, this book represents the voice of the children and young people through quotes and case studies throughout.

Emotionally based school avoidance

Emotionally Based School Avoidance Toolkit www.westsussex.gov.uk/local-offer/information/education/emotionally-based-school-avoidance-ebsa

The Educational Psychology Service in West Sussex have developed some excellent resources for schools and parents to work together to support children in attending school.

Understanding and supporting Children and Young People with Emotionally Based School Avoidance (EBSA) (by Tina Rae)

A practical guide to understanding and supporting young people with EBSA. The Sunday Evening, Monday Morning plan, and other photocopiable resources, may be particularly helpful to teaching assistants.

School Wellbeing Card Set (by Dr Jerricah Holder) www.schoolwellbeingcards.co.uk

These cards can be used to help children struggling with EBSA to express their feelings, identify risks and protective factors. There are versions for children and adolescents.

Suicide

Papyrus UK www.papyrus-uk.org

Papyrus is a charity that works to prevent young suicide. They have produced a number of useful publications for school staff to refer to in the prevention of suicide, and also postvention should the worst happen in your school setting.

Samaritans www.samaritans.org

Confidential, free support 24/7 through their crisis line. They also provide helpful resources such as a safety plan template.

Zero Suicide Alliance www.zerosuicidealliance.com

Provides free training for school staff on supporting young people with suicidal thoughts.

Stay Alive app www.stayalive.app

This app can be downloaded by students so that they can carry their safety plan with them wherever they go. They can also access crisis support and a 'Life Box', in which they can save life-affirming photographs to provide reassurance and hope when it is needed most.

Self-care

Anna Freud Centre www.annafreud.org/on-my-mind/self-care

Lots of self-care ideas so that you can find what works for you.

Calm www.calm.com/schools/resources

The Calm app contains meditations, sleep stories, and calming music and soundscapes to help you to relax. They specifically recognize the stressful role of those who work in schools and have developed a self-care guide to help you to take care of yourself.

Mentally Healthy Schools www.mentallyhealthyschools.org.uk

Mentally Healthy Schools, together with the Anna Freud Centre, have developed self-care resources for primary and secondary staff to use with students and also for themselves.

Peer supervision

Barnardo's: *Supervision in Education – Healthier Schools for All* www. barnardos.org.uk/sites/default/files/uploads/Supervision%20in%20 Education%20-%20Healthier%20Schools%20For%20All%20-%20 Main%20report_0.pdf

A report exploring experiences of supervision amongst school staff in Scotland.

The Wisdom of Crowds (by James Surowiecki)

An inspirational and accessible book about the value of using many heads together to problem-solve.

Appendix 1: List of Acronyms, Abbreviations and Key Terms

As a member of staff in a school, you will encounter a great deal of professional jargon in your job. This list/glossary of relevant wellbeing and mental health key terms will help you to both understand these terms and explain them to others.

ADD/ADHD – attention deficit (and hyperactivity) disorder. Syndromes which may exhibit extreme impulsiveness, inattentiveness and continuous motor activity.

Annual review – a meeting held annually to review a pupil's education, health and care plan (EHCP). The EHCP will be looked at closely by all the professionals involved. The pupil's parents, and often the pupil, will be invited to attend. Everyone discusses how the learner is progressing and agrees any changes that may be needed in the provision that is being offered. Everyone needs to agree whether to continue with the current provision, request more provision, suggest changes, reduce the provision or cease maintaining the EHCP. All of this must be appropriately recorded.

ASD/ASC – autistic spectrum disorder or condition. This is a neurodevelopmental condition that impacts how a person perceives and socializes with others.

CAMHS – Child and Adolescent Mental Health Service. Local multidisciplinary services promoting the mental health and psychological wellbeing of children and young people and supporting their families.

CBT – cognitive behavioural therapy; looks at the interaction between thoughts, feelings and behaviours.

Counselling – counselling allows children and young people time to discuss their problems and concerns. Counselling services vary in different parts of the country. Many areas have local information services where young people and their families can seek advice. Some counselling services are made available through schools, but this depends on the type of training that has been undertaken by the counsellor.

CYP – children and young people.

DSL – designated safeguarding lead. This is the person who leads on safeguarding within a school. They are supported by deputy designated safeguarding leads.

DDSL – deputy designated safeguarding lead. This role involves supporting the designated safeguarding lead to ensure that children within the school are safe from harm.

EBSA/EBSNA – emotionally based school avoidance/emotionally based school non-attendance. The favoured terms currently used to describe children who are unable to attend school due to their emotions.

EP – educational psychologist. Educational psychologists work with children and young people, parents and staff, using psychology to help to understand thoughts, feelings and behaviours, with the aim of improving educational outcomes and wellbeing.

EHCP – education, health and care plan. The document issued by the local authority which contains details of the child's educational needs, as identified by the local authority during the statutory assessment. The EHCP includes details of the provision required to meet those needs. It names the school that the child will attend (agreed with the parents and the school). Usually, this will be the school the child already attends, but occasionally a special school is considered to be more suitable.

ELSA – emotional literacy support assistant. A member of staff trained and supervised by an educational psychologist to deliver emotional literacy interventions.

EMHP – education mental health practitioners promote emotional wellbeing in educational settings and deliver interventions. They work within local mental health support teams.

EOTAS – education other than at school. EOTAS includes hospital school, online schooling or home tuition. Local authorities are advised by the government to consider providing part-time education to a child if full-time education would not be in their best interests for physical or mental health reasons. The local authorities should determine the basis of education that would be in the child's best interests.

Family therapy – a way of helping individuals overcome problems within the context of the family unit. These problems may affect more than one family member, so therapy addresses the way that they interact with each other. Family therapists are often psychotherapists.

FSW – family support worker. Often accessed through an Early Help referral to Children's Services.

Gillick competence – this term refers to the circumstances under which young people may receive help without parental consent or knowledge.

Graduated approach – the SEND Code of Practice states that schools should follow a graduated approach when providing SEN support. This is based on a cycle of 'Assess, Plan, Do, Review'.

High needs funding/high needs top-up funding – high needs funding is the funding that local authorities use to pay for special school places. High needs top-up funding is additional funding paid directly by the local authority for some pupils with high needs.

Hyperactivity – the inability to focus on one task for a period of time, and the need to be constantly on the move.

Hypoactivity – the opposite of hyperactivity. Children who are hypoactive, though also unable to concentrate, often appear to be in a daze and to lack energy.

IEP – individual education plan. The plan devised for meeting a learner's special educational needs. It is prepared specially for the learner concerned. It sets out what support will be given in the following weeks, who will provide it and what resources will be required. It also sets out specific targets for the learner. IEPs are usually reviewed by the school every term or half term, or more often if required. Parents and pupils are invited to discuss and review the plan and to help decide new targets.

Impulsivity – this is when children react to a situation without considering the consequences.

Inclusion – inclusion is about creating an appropriate learning environment for all children. It involves introducing policies and practices that enable pupils with learning difficulties and disabilities to participate fully in school life. The process of inclusion should involve a regular critical evaluation of school policies and practices to ensure that quality learning opportunities are available to all, whatever their needs.

LA – local authority. The LA is a synthesis of all children's services, including education and social services.

LAC – looked after child. A term used to describe those children who are in the care of the local authority or children's social services.

LSA – learning support assistant.

Mainstream school – a school providing education for all children, whether or not they have special educational needs or disabilities.

MHL – mental health lead, also known more formally as senior lead for mental health (SLMH). Usually a member of the leadership team within school who oversees the whole-school approach to mental health.

MHST – mental health support teams are multidisciplinary teams working in local areas to deliver support to schools.

OCD – obsessive compulsive disorder.

ODD – oppositional defiant disorder.

OT – occupational therapy/therapist.

Outcome – outcomes describe the difference that will be made to a child or young person as a result of special educational and other provision. These must be specific, measurable, achievable, realistic and time-bound (SMART).

PDA – pathological demand avoidance. A pattern of behaviour recognized as being part of the autism spectrum. There is some debate among clinicians as to whether PDA comprises a separate condition to autism, or rather describes a collection of symptoms of autism; therefore, it is currently inconsistently given as a separate diagnosis.

PEP – personal education plan. A plan that is drawn up for looked after children and focuses on their educational needs. It is usually reviewed at the same time as the care plan.

PMHW – primary mental health workers provide specialist CAMHS skills and knowledge within the wider community (e.g. schools).

PRU – pupil referral unit. The aim of pupil referral units is to get pupils back into the mainstream school. These units are set up and maintained by the local authority and provide education for children who are unable to attend a mainstream school (e.g. excluded children or children with EBSA).

PSP – pastoral support plan. A PSP should be set up for any disaffected pupil or one at risk of permanent exclusion. It should detail interventions to help pupils manage their behaviour. A PSP should set realistic targets for the pupil to work towards that have been agreed with the parents/carers.

Resourced or resource provision – resourced provision within mainstream schools is where pupils are either withdrawn to a resource for specialist input, or teachers from the resource deliver specialist help to the child within the classroom. A resource provision usually has a specialist focus, such as hearing impairment, autism or speech and language needs.

School support staff – a term that is used to describe a wide range of adults who have supporting roles in schools, and may include teaching assistants, technicians, administrative staff, librarians, midday supervisors and many more.

Self-esteem – this describes how positively (high self-esteem) or negatively (low self-esteem) children perceive themselves within their environment.

SEMH – social, emotional and mental health needs.

SEN/SEND – special educational needs/special educational needs and disabilities. SEN (or SEND) is a term used to describe conditions that make it more difficult for a child to learn in comparison to other children of the same age.

SENCo/SENDCo – special educational needs coordinator/special educational needs and disabilities coordinator. A SENCo (or SENDCo) is a qualified teacher who has responsibility for coordinating SEND provision.

SEND Code of Practice – the document, published by the government in 2014, setting out the statutory duties of local authorities, schools, early education settings and health and social services. It provides a framework for the identification and assessment of children with special needs. It also provides guidelines for making effective provision for these children.

SENDisT – special educational needs and disability tribunal.

Sensory impairment – a sensory impairment can be described as an impairment of any of the five senses (e.g. visual or hearing impairment).

Sensory-motor – the relationship between sensation and movement.

SMHL – senior mental health lead, also known less formally as mental health lead (MHL). Usually a member of the leadership team within school who oversees the whole-school approach to mental health.

Special school – a school specially organized and designed to support pupils with a statement of special educational needs. Some special schools cater predominantly for one area of learning difficulty or disability. There are usually specialist teachers and resources on site and children are taught in small groups.

SSRI – selective serotonin re-uptake inhibitor. This is a type of antidepressant medication.

Statutory assessment – the process which takes place if the local authority believes that it needs to outline the child's needs, at the request of the school, parent or another agency. It does not always lead to an EHCP. The authority looks at all that has been done for the child, reports from professionals and previous IEPs. An educational psychologist assesses the child and prepares a report. A panel within the local authority considers all the evidence and decides whether to give an EHCP.

SWOT analysis – a problem-solving framework involving the analysis of the strengths, weaknesses, opportunities and threats of a given situation.

TA – teaching assistant.

Tactile – relating to the sense of touch.

Tolerable stress – the way that the body responds to prolonged high levels of stress with the support from a sensitive caregiver to soothe them and help to regulate the stress response. With this support, the stress is tolerated and can easily return to a normal state.

Toxic stress – the way that the body responds to prolonged high levels of stress, without support from a sensitive caregiver to help to regulate the stress response and soothe the child. This chronic stress, often resulting from abuse and neglect, impacts on brain development and can cause lifelong health problems.

Appendix 2: Format for Reflective Learning Log

✳ Date:.......................
   Incident to be reflected on: ....

What happened?	
What were you thinking/ feeling?	
What was good/bad about the experience?	

cont.

What sense can you make of the situation?	
What else could you have done?	
If the situation arose again, what would you do?	

Appendix 3: Format for Recording Peer Supervision Notes

✳ Supervision date: ....

　Attendees: ....

Before supervision: What would you like to bring to the supervision session? What would you like to gain from the supervision session?	
During supervision: Notes from the session	

cont.

After supervision:
What did you learn in supervision? What can you do as next steps?

Date of next supervision session:..

Appendix 4: 'Concerned About a Pupil's Mental Health' Flowchart

Is the child in immediate danger?

NO → Have they come to speak to you and/or are they in obvious distress?

YES → Call 999. Follow safeguarding policy and first aid protocol.

From "Have they come to speak to you...":

NO → Gather information and prepare. Discuss with MHL and/or DSL. Decide who should speak to them, when and where. Make a written record of concerns.

YES → Find a quiet place to talk to the young person.

Find a quiet place to talk to the young person.
↓
Discuss outcome with MHL and/or DSL and make a written record.
↓
Discuss with primary caregivers wherever possible, following safeguarding policy.
↓
Decide on next steps for signposting and support using the THRIVE Framework.

Appendix 5: FIRES Framework Poster

FAST RESPONSE	IDENTIFY NEEDS AND RISKS	REASSURE	EMPATHIZE AND LISTEN	SUPPORT AND SIGNPOST
Act quickly when you notice possible signs of mental distress.	Assess the situation for immediate needs and for risk of harm.	Stay calm, unshockable and provide reassurance.	Listen non-judgementally, validate, accept and empathize.	Offer support strategies, pass on information and refer for professional support.